W9-BOF-174

Principles

Short Essays on Ethics

Principles

Short Essays on Ethics

Second Edition

Thomas Hurka

University of Calgary

HARCOURT
BRACE
CANADA

Harcourt Brace & Company, Canada

Toronto Montreal Fort Worth New York Orlando
Philadelphia San Diego London Sydney Tokyo

Requests for permission to photocopy any part of this work should be sent in writing to: College Licensing Officer, Cancopy, 6 Adelaide Street East, Suite 900, Toronto, ON, M5C 1H6. Fax: (416) 868-1621. All other inquiries should be directed to the publisher.

Every reasonable effort has been made to acquire permission for copyright material used in this text, and to acknowledge all such indebtedness accu-rately. Any errors or omissions called to the publisher's attention will be corrected in future printings.

Canadian Cataloguing in Publication Data
Hurka, Thomas, 1952–
    Principles : short essays on ethics

2nd ed.
ISBN 0–7747–3634–8

1. Ethics.   I. Title.
BJ1012.H87   1999   170   C98–932580–6

New Editions Editor: *Megan Mueller*
Developmental Editor: *Camille Isaacs*
Production Editor: *Carolyn McLarty*
Senior Production Co-ordinator: *Sue-Ann Becker*
Copy Editor/Proofreader: *Sharlene Weaver*
Cover and Interior Design: *The Brookview Group Inc.*
Typesetting and Assembly: *Carolyn Hutchings*
Printing and Binding: *Hignell Printing Limited*

Cover Art: Juan Gonzalez, *Rembrandt's Hands, Vermeer's Frame and the Passing of the Moth* (1990). Oil and acrylic on honeycomb panel, 33 x 29 inches. Image provided by the Nancy Hoffman Gallery, New York. Reproduced with per-mission of the artist's family.

Harcourt Brace & Company Canada, Ltd.
55 Horner Avenue, Toronto, ON, Canada M8Z 4X6.
Customer Service
Toll-Free Tel.: 1-800-387-7278
Toll-Free fax: 1-800-665-7307

This book was printed in Canada.
1 2 3 4 5   03 02 01 00 99

Preface

When *The Globe and Mail* invited me to write a weekly ethics column, I was surprised and excited. I had long thought there ought to be a column of this kind in a Canadian newspaper, and planned to propose one to *The Globe* at some time in the future. What I wanted to do they were now approaching me about.

Philosophical ethics has many merits: its methods allow clearer formulations of ethical issues and progress in resolving them. But it is largely ignored in public debates; when politicians, activists, and editorialists discuss ethical issues, they often show what to a philosopher is a lamentable lack of rigour, sophistication, and even intellectual honesty. If it matters that these issues be debated properly, it matters that the philosophical approach to them become more widely known.

This was my guiding aim in writing for *The Globe*. I always cared less about persuading readers of my particular conclusion in a column than about displaying, through a series of columns, what I see as the distinctive features of philosophical ethics. I wanted to show that ethical issues can be discussed dispassionately rather than rhetorically, with precision and care in argumentation. I wanted to describe views opposed to my own fairly, even highlighting their plausibility, rather than with sarcastic misrepresentation. Above all, I wanted to focus on ethical principles. Philosophical ethics is systematic, connecting claims on particular issues to general principles that explain and justify them, and which imply parallel claims on other, superficially different topics. As far as possible in 700–900 words, I wanted to show the merits of this systematic approach to ethics.

At the same time, the columns had to be tailored to a newspaper audience. Their language had to be accessible and lively, and their pacing brisk. (No pausing to answer four objections to a claim.) It was vital to have a catchy lead paragraph to grab readers' interest, and to tie a column to recent events in the news. Humour was absolutely an asset. And the columns had to have an opinion. As my editor told me when I began writing, a newspaper column can't set out the arguments on both sides of an issue and leave the reader to decide between them. It has to "help" the reader by stating an opinion — and the stronger the opinion, the better.

I was surprised how much philosophy could be done within these constraints — both how much I could write and how much the newspaper would let through. And over time I came to value the constraints. It's worthwhile to write about abstract issues in a less formal, more accessible way. If philosophical ethics has little influence outside academe, it's partly because we philosophers don't write about it non-academically. And what goes for newspaper readers goes also for our students: hence this book.

Principles: Short Essays on Ethics, Second Edition, is intended as a text for introductory philosophy courses, especially ethics courses, and for intermediate courses in contemporary moral problems.

It isn't meant to replace traditional anthologies of philosophical articles, which will remain central tools for teaching. But it can supplement them in several ways.

First, it can provide accessible introductory readings on ethical issues. The articles in traditional anthologies are usually drawn from philosophy journals, where their intended audience was professional philosophers. It's important that our students learn to understand these articles, but it's not clear that such articles make the best initial reading on a topic. Recognizing this, some anthology editors include selections from more popular sources, such as magazines and politicians' speeches, but many instructors find these selections insufficiently philosophical. The essays in this book can provide readable introductions to ethical issues that are also attuned to philosophical concerns: while popular in style, they aim at rigour in content. On a more pragmatic note, if the first reading on a topic is a 700–900 word essay, it is one an instructor can realistically expect every student attending a class to have read.

Second, the volume can tie abstract issues to specific examples from the news: Dr. Kevorkian's "suicide machine," the Gulf War, the exclusion of blacks at a particular U.S. golf club. Students often discuss issues best with specific examples before them, which the essays can provide.

Finally, the volume can expand the range covered by anthologies. With 59 essays, it discusses more topics than a traditional anthology and can provide readings on topics, such as surrogate motherhood and vegetarianism, that may not appear in one's main text. It has an introduction to philosophical ethics addressed to beginning students, and the brevity of its essays may tempt students to browse philosophically. (An instructor receiving late essays may wish to recommend the essay on procrastination.)

The essays are divided into parts thematically. Seven parts — on cultural identities, biomedical ethics, the environment, economic distribution, equality and discrimination, personal life, and violence and war — are on topics in applied ethics; they are suitable for contemporary moral problems courses and for the part of an introductory course that discusses moral problems. Three parts — on the nature of morality, the good life, and virtues and vices — address more theoretical topics, such as religion and ethics, relativism, and the value of pleasure. They are suitable for the theoretical segment of a survey course on ethics or for the opening part of a contemporary problems course. The book contains a variety of essays in a variety of styles, and will, I hope, be helpful to students in many philosophy courses.

ACKNOWLEDGEMENTS

Many of the essays in this volume first appeared as columns in *The Globe and Mail,* under the standing title "Principles." I am grateful to *The Globe's* editor-in-chief, William Thorsell, for conceiving the idea of a weekly ethics column, and to Chris Waddell and John Allemang for thinking I might be the person to write it.

As the columns were being written, they were edited first by my wife Terry Teskey and then by Phil Jackman at *The Globe.* Both saved me from numerous inelegances, and Phil added excellent headlines, many of which are retained in this book.

"Philosophy, Morality, and *The English Patient*" first appeared in *Queen's Quarterly,* Spring 1997, pp. 3 – 11. It is reproduced here with the permission of *Queen's Quarterly.*

Michael Young at Harcourt Brace & Company, Canada conceived the idea of this book; his reader, Thomas O'Connor, supported the project and made helpful suggestions. I am grateful to them both. The impetus for the second edition came from Megan Mueller and Camille Isaacs of Harcourt Brace, who also provided helpful advice about needed revisions.

My largest debt is to the community of moral philosophers. The essays in this volume do not, for the most part, contain original ideas. They try to summarize conclusions that have emerged from debates among philosophers in books and journal articles, and in a more academic setting would be full of footnotes. Like other branches of philosophy, ethics is a co-operative endeavour. We move forward by criticizing others' theses and trying to improve upon them. To the many who have participated in this endeavour, and whose ideas I have tried to convey to a wider public, I am above all grateful.

A NOTE FROM THE PUBLISHER

Thank you for selecting the second edition of *Principles: Short Essays on Ethics* by Thomas Hurka. The author and publisher have devoted considerable time to the careful development of this book. We appreciate your recognition of this effort and accomplishment.

We want to hear what you think about *Principles: Short Essays on Ethics*. Please take a few minutes to fill in the stamped reply card that you will find at the back of the book. Your comments, suggestions, and criticisms will be valuable to us as we prepare new editions and other books.

Contents

Part One
Cultural Identities

Part Two
Biomedical Ethics

Part Three
Environmental Ethics

Part Four
The Nature of Morality

Part Five
Justice and Economic Distribution

Part Six
The Good Life

Part Seven
Equality and Discrimination

Part Eight
Ethics of Personal Life

Part Nine
Violence and War

Part Ten
Virtues and Vices

Introduction

*P*eople disagree about ethical issues, and we also argue about them. By this I don't mean that we raise our voices and call each other names. I mean that we try to persuade each other of ethical conclusions by giving reasons or justifications for them. You do or should believe this, we say, from which it follows that abortion is a woman's right or capital punishment is just or whatever ethical conclusion we're defending. We try to establish ethical conclusions by pointing to reasons that support them.

These practices show several things about how we understand ethical issues. That we disagree at all shows that we think there are correct conclusions on these issues that everyone should accept. We don't buy the "relativist" line that what's right for a person depends on what he thinks is right; if we did, we wouldn't see our different ethical opinions as clashing. (See the essay, "Values Are *Not* Relative," below.) In addition, that we argue about ethical issues shows that we think they can be resolved rationally and can even become the object of a rational consensus. Our ethical opinions aren't just unchangeable prejudices but can be reasoned about and improved. The use of ethical argument therefore makes optimistic assumptions about the prospects for ethical thought. But though such argument is in general a good thing, there are better and worse versions of it. Unfortunately, what we most often see are the less satisfactory kinds.

The most common forum for ethical argument is a debate between politicians or advocates for different sides of an issue on a TV talk show. This format gives participants an over-riding interest in winning, which in turn makes them behave more like high school debaters or courtroom lawyers than like people trying to reach a reasoned agreement. Let me illustrate by considering one well-known issue, capital punishment.

This hasn't been a live political issue in Canada since 1987, when the House of Commons voted to continue the country's ban on capital punishment. But it's an issue on which many people have firm views and that's regularly in the news, if only because of its widespread use in the United States. It's also an issue where the general lines of debate are fairly well known.

Each side of the capital punishment debate presents a series of arguments for its position. Thus, abolitionists say that capital punishment involves the deliberate taking of human life, which is always wrong; that it's no better at deterring murder than is life imprisonment; and that it involves the terrible risk of executing an innocent person. Proponents reply that capital punishment can be a demand of justice — some criminals deserve to die. In addition, capital punishment does deter better than life imprisonment and is less expensive than maintaining a criminal at public expense for up to 25 years.

Each side also tries to rebut the other's arguments, or to show that they don't hold water. But the working assumption is that the side with more arguments, or more unrefuted arguments, wins. If one side has three points standing at the end of the debate while the other has two, the first side has established its case.

Though it's common enough, this approach to ethical argument is in several ways unsatisfying. First, merely counting the arguments on the two sides ignores the fact that some arguments have more ethical weight than others. Consider the pro-capital punishment argument about saving money. Surely it counts less than arguments about justice or killing; when lives are at stake, dollars and cents aren't that important. Second, counting arguments one by one leaves aside questions about how they relate to our other ethical views. Consider the anti-capital punishment argument that all deliberate killing is wrong. How does it relate to the widespread view that killing in self-defence, which can also be deliberate, is not always wrong? Does the argument require us to change our view about self-defence? If not, how does it differentiate between punishment and self-defence? Why is one kind of deliberate killing wrong but the other not?

Finally, merely counting arguments ignores questions about whether the arguments on a given side add up to a consistent whole. These questions may not matter much in other argumentative contexts. A lawyer defending a client against a murder charge can argue, first, that her client wasn't at the scene of the crime; second, that even if he was at the scene he didn't kill the victim; and, third, that even if he did kill the victim it was justified self-defence. If the jury are persuaded by one of these arguments, they can ignore the fact that it's inconsistent with the other two. But this kind of inconsistency is more troubling in ethical contexts. Consider the pro-capital punishment argument that the death penalty deters better than life imprisonment. Doesn't it suggest that if capital punishment *didn't* deter better it *wouldn't* be right? How does this relate to the argument that capital punishment is in itself a demand of justice? To sharpen this issue, imagine that capital punishment somehow encouraged murder, so there were more killings of innocent people with it than without. Would the defender of capital punishment still favour it because of justice or oppose it because of its effects? Similar questions arise about the anti-capital punishment argument that the death penalty is not a better deterrent. Doesn't it suggest that if capital punishment *were* a better deterrent, it *would* be right? How does this relate to the argument that all deliberate killing is wrong? How also does it relate to the argument about executing an innocent person? Imagine that capital punishment would prevent ten murders of innocent people every year but would also, predictably but unavoidably, mistakenly execute one innocent person. Would it then be right because of its overall effects or wrong because of the one tragic error?

If we ask these questions, we are moving to a different, more philosophical approach to ethical issues. This approach is less interested in winning a debate than in arriving at an ethical conclusion that is correct or best justified. Because of this, it considers arguments not just on one side of an issue but on both sides, so long as the arguments are serious and merit attention. Moreover, it considers these arguments in a special way. It's interested in arriving at the ethical conclusion that's best supported by general ethical reasons or principles, and it therefore tries to discover what those principles are. What general principles explain why and when punishment of any kind is ethically right, and how do those principles apply to the specific case of capital punishment? Even more generally, what principles explain why and when action of any kind is right, and what do they say about capital punishment? The aim in this approach to ethical issues isn't to establish a particular conclusion that you're committed to from the start by using whatever arguments are handy. It's to identify the best conclusion possible by deriving it from fundamental ethical principles. This philosophical approach doesn't make settling ethical issues a snap. This might be so if everyone agreed on fundamental principles, so deciding about, say, capital punishment was just a matter of seeing how our shared commitments apply to it. But in fact people disagree as much about principles as about specific issues. What some of us think is a fundamental ethical principle others see as false, and vice versa. But there's still a lot to be gained from looking at general principles, if only because differences on these are fewer in number. While there are dozens of disagreements about capital punishment, abortion, war, and other issues, there are only a few about principles. And the latter disagreements often underlie the former. If we examine the debates about capital punishment and similar issues, we find that they often turn on the same abstract differences about which general considerations are most ethically important. This helps us understand the more concrete debates, because it shows us how much they have in common. It also points us to where ethical consensus is most likely to be found. If we could agree on the general principles, then, assuming we could agree on facts such as whether capital punishment deters better than life imprisonment, we could agree on a whole range of ethical issues.

So what are the main disagreements about ethical principles? These are best understood as disagreements between three general approaches to ethical questions, or three general ethical theories. Each of these theories is believed, or at least followed roughly, by many people. Each is also based on an initially plausible ethical idea. I call these theories *consequentialism, Judeo-Christian morality*, and *libertarianism*.

Consequentialism starts from the simple, and to many people compelling, idea that if an action has good consequences — if it brings about good things or prevents bad ones — this counts ethically in favour of the action. Consequentialism makes this one idea the only fundamental idea, so the evaluation of actions is always in terms of their consequences. The ethically right action is always the one with the best overall consequences, or the one that will produce the greatest surplus of good over evil in the world as a whole.

This theory obviously needs an account of what makes consequences good or bad, and here there are several possibilities. Presumably some central goods and evils are states of human beings, so right actions tend to make human lives better and wrong ones to make them worse. Some people think the only ethical good is happiness, understood variously as pleasure or getting what you want, and the only evil is unhappiness, understood as pain or frustration. This view leads to a specific version of consequentialism called *utilitarianism*, according to which what is right is always what produces the most happiness, or, more precisely, the greatest surplus of happiness over unhappiness, in the world. Utilitarians care centrally about human happiness, but many also value the happiness of animals. (See "Why Many Find Meat-Eating Hard to Digest," below.) It may be that animals cannot experience as rich or intense forms of happiness as humans, in which case their lives have less value than human lives. But in so far as they can experience pleasure and pain, their doing so has the same value, and does the same to make acts right, as the similar pleasure and pain of humans.

Against this utilitarian view, some consequentialists deny that the only good is happiness and the only evil unhappiness. They insist that a world in which everyone experienced only simple bodily pleasures, a world like the one described in Aldous Huxley's *Brave New World*, would not be ethically best or what we ought to bring about. (See "Pleasure Alone Won't Make You Happy," below.) According to these *perfectionists*, there are more important human goods than happiness, goods such as knowledge, achievement, self-direction, virtue, and love. The best life, and the one we should try to help people to live, is not the happiest but the one that contains the most of these higher human goods. Once again similar goods can be found in animals, as they develop their distinctive species natures or achieve the excellences appropriate to their kinds.

Yet other consequentialists value goods that aren't states of individual humans or animals. For example, some value equality in the distribution of goods such as happiness. They say a slightly smaller quantity of happiness that is equally divided can be better than a larger quantity that is concentrated on just a few people. Yet others value distributions according to desert. They say it's especially good when a virtuous person is happy, because then the happiness is not only good in itself but also deserved, and bad when a vicious person is happy. Analogously, it's especially bad when a virtuous person suffers pain but good when a vicious person does. Here there is another good, desert, to be used in calculating the overall goodness of consequences and the rightness and wrongness of acts.

Whatever its account of good and evil, consequentialism can only be applied if we know what the consequences of actions will be. To know for certain what even the simplest consequentialist theory, utilitarianism, deems right, we must know how much happiness and unhappiness the various actions available to us will cause all the people in the world — something we can never know precisely. This isn't, however, a decisive objection to consequentialism. If there are cases where we can't know which action will have the best consequences, then in these cases we have to say, as it's sometimes perfectly reasonable to say, that we can't know which actions are right and wrong. And in many cases we can know which action will or is likely to have the best consequences. For example, if a U.S. President decided to launch a nuclear attack on Canada just for his own amusement, that would clearly do more harm than good and be ethically wrong. And even on less clear-cut issues, consequentialism has distinctive implications about which kinds of consideration are ethically most important. We can see this by returning to the issue of capital punishment.

Most versions of consequentialism make the crucial arguments about capital punishment the ones about deterrence. If capital punishment is a sufficiently better deterrent than life imprisonment, it's ethically right; if it's not a better deterrent, it's probably ethically wrong. This is certainly true of utilitarianism, where deterrence is important because of its effects on happiness. By killing the convicted criminal, capital punishment deprives him of the (perhaps limited) happiness he would enjoy if he stayed alive in prison, which would make it wrong if it had no compensating good effects. But if capital punishment also prevents the murders of several innocent people, it does more good by preserving their happiness than it does by killing the criminal, and it also promotes the happiness of people generally by allowing them a greater sense of security. So it can be on balance right. Utilitarianism gives no weight to the argument that capital punishment is required in itself by justice; nothing is required in itself, apart from its effects on happiness. It likewise gives no weight to the argument that all deliberate killing is wrong. Though killing usually has bad effects on its victim, some killing has greater good effects on other people, as self-defence killing does, and capital punishment can if it's a sufficient deterrent. Finally, utilitarianism gives no special weight to the argument that capital punishment can sometimes execute an innocent person. This person's loss of life is indeed a harm, but this harm is outweighed if enough other innocent people's lives are saved by the deterrence of murder. What matters is only the total effects of capital punishment, of which mistaken executions are only one.

Despite the complexity of applying it in practice, consequentialism is at the theoretical level extremely simple. It contains just one fundamental principle, saying that what's right is always what will have the best consequences. Some philosophers think this makes consequentialism too simple. More specifically, they say consequentialism goes wrong by sometimes demanding too much of people and sometimes allowing too much.

Because it requires us always to do what will produce the *most* good, consequentialism is an extremely demanding ethical theory. Consider the duty to help others, say, by contributing to charity. Consequentialism makes this a duty not just to contribute some money to charity, but to keep contributing so long as this will do more good to others than harm to ourselves. But if a unit of money always does more good to someone with less than to someone with more (see "Some Taxing Questions about Wealth," below), this is a very onerous duty. If there are millions of people starving in the developing world, and they'll get more from a dollar than anyone who isn't starving, we have a duty to keep giving until we reduce ourselves to starvation. Critics of consequentialism say this is far too onerous a duty. Even if people have some duty to help others, this duty has limits. It may require them to contribute something to charity, but it also allows them, if they choose, to care somewhat more about their own lives and interests.

At the same time, consequentialism places no limits on the means that are used to produce good consequences. Whatever action has the best results is right, however it produces those results; no actions are wrong in themselves. Consequentialism can therefore approve actions that many people will think are horribly morally wrong.

Consider an example involving capital punishment. In a small town in the southern United States earlier this century, a white woman has just claimed she's been raped by a black man. You're the sheriff of this town and have no evidence against any rapist and even doubt whether a rape actually occurred. But the whites of the town have told you that unless you convict someone quickly they'll take matters into their own hands. They'll start a riot, lynch several black men, and cause extensive further damage. As you see things, you have only one option. The only way you can stop the riot and lynchings is to fabricate evidence against an innocent black man and execute him. This will of course cost that man his life, but it will save the lives of several black men and prevent the decades of animosity that will follow if the riot goes ahead. Should you frame and execute the innocent black man? If you can do so without being found out, consequentialism says you should. But many people would find this horribly wrong. Even though your action would have good consequences, even the best possible, it would violate the innocent man's right not to be treated unjustly and is therefore forbidden. It may often be the case that the action with the best consequences is right, so in those cases the end justifies the means. But this isn't always so. Sometimes the means required to achieve a good end are in themselves forbidden and producing that end is on balance wrong.

The second ethical theory, or general approach to ethics, accepts these criticisms of consequentialism. Unfortunately, it has no universally accepted name. Some call it *common-sense morality*, because it's the morality most of us were brought up in and use in everyday life. Others call it *Judeo-Christian morality*, because it has roots in Jewish and Christian ethical teaching. (Some people affirm this morality on a specifically religious basis, but others take it to be broadly correct even though they're not themselves religious.) But its structure is very different from that of consequentialism. Whereas consequentialism contains just one fundamental principle or duty, Judeo-Christian morality (as I will call it) contains many duties. Some of these duties apply in different areas of life; for example, one concerns killing and another telling the truth. But often different duties can apply to the same action, with one tending to make it right and the other to make it wrong. In these cases, Judeo-Christian morality must decide which of the competing duties is stronger. If an action fulfils one relatively minor duty but violates another major one, the action is on balance forbidden.

Judeo-Christian morality agrees with consequentialism that there's an ethical duty to produce good consequences, both for oneself and for others. And this duty again requires an account of what makes consequences good, which can be utilitarian, perfectionist, or something different. But the Judeo-Christian duty to produce good consequences is less demanding than the consequentialist duty, because it doesn't require us always to produce what's best. On the contrary, Judeo-Christian morality allows us, if we wish, to refuse to make sacrifices for others if they'll be significantly harmful to ourselves. If we do nothing at all for others, we do violate an important duty. But if we stop short of doing the most possible for them, we fail to be saintly or heroic but don't do something positively wrong. We have some duties to contribute to charities benefitting the starving, but not to the point of starving ourselves.

At the same time, Judeo-Christian morality contains many other duties forbidding certain actions apart from their consequences. Thus, it contains duties forbidding killing the innocent, lying, breaking promises, and stealing just because of the types of actions those are. This morality therefore disagrees with consequentialism about the example of the riot in the southern U.S. town. It says that even though framing and executing the innocent man would have the best consequences, it's ethically wrong because it violates the duty not to kill. In *absolutist* versions of Judeo-Christian morality, the forbidden actions may never be performed no matter how good their consequences. Killing the innocent and lying are wrong always and without exception, even if they're necessary to avoid absolute disaster. In *non-absolutist* versions, however, these actions may be permitted if their consequences are sufficiently better than the alternatives'. Perhaps executing an innocent person isn't allowed to save just five or ten innocent lives, but is allowed if it's the only way to save thousands or millions. In all versions of Judeo-Christian morality, however, the evaluation of actions doesn't turn just on their consequences. Though the end may sometimes justify the means, as when an action produces good consequences without violating any other duty, it doesn't always do so. Sometimes the action with the best consequences is, despite that fact, on balance wrong.

The prohibitions of Judeo-Christian morality are expressed in a series of distinct duties, about killing the innocent, lying, and so on. But they have a common structure, as we can see by looking more closely at the example of the southern riot.

In this example you have two options: execute the innocent man and save the people who'd be killed in a riot, or spare the innocent man and let those people die. The first option has the best overall consequences, but its consequences include something bad: the innocent man's death. And there are two facts about the way it produces this bad consequence that lead Judeo-Christian morality to find it ethically wrong.

First, if you frame and execute the innocent man, his death results from something you *did* — from some positive action you took. But if you spare that man, the deaths in the riot don't result from any action of yours. They result from what you didn't do, or are something you merely allowed to happen. And Judeo-Christian morality believes that causing a bad consequence by a positive action is worse than allowing it to come about, or that causing harm is worse than merely allowing it. (See "Euthanasia: Dr. Kevorkian's Suicide Machine," below.) In this example, causing one innocent death by killing is worse than allowing several innocent deaths that you could have prevented if you had killed.

Second, if you execute the innocent man, his death is something you *intend*, if not as your goal than at least as a means to your goal. Your goal is the good one of saving several lives. But you intend to achieve that goal by killing the innocent man, so his death is intended by you as a means. It's part of your plan, rather than just a side effect of carrying it out. But you don't intend the deaths of the riot victims in the same way if you refuse to execute the innocent man. You may know the deaths will follow, so they're something you foresee. But in this case the deaths aren't part of your plan. They're neither your goal nor a means to your goal, since you aren't saving the innocent man *by* allowing the others to die. And Judeo-Christian morality holds that intending a bad consequence as a goal or means to your goal is worse than merely foreseeing that it will come about, or that intending harm is worse than merely foreseeing it. (See "Morality and War: How to Fight," below.) In the riot example, intending one innocent death is worse than merely foreseeing the several deaths that will result from your failure to kill.

The riot example is a favourable one for Judeo-Christian morality, because in it these two distinctions work together. One option involves bringing about a bad consequence in a way that's worse on both counts — it involves causing a death rather than merely allowing it, and intending the death rather than merely foreseeing it. The other option involves bringing about bad consequences in a way that's less bad on both counts, so the two distinctions support each other. This is also the case in several other examples. Imagine that you're a surgeon with five patients needing transplants, each of a different organ. There are no donors, and if you do nothing all five patients will die within an hour. But you can kidnap a vagrant on the street, kill her, and divide her organs among the five. If you can do this undetected, consequentialism seems to say it's right. But Judeo-Christian morality again disagrees. If you kill the vagrant, her death both results from something you did and is intended by you as a means. But if you don't kill the vagrant, you merely allow the patients to die and merely foresee their deaths. Though not killing the vagrant may have overall worse consequences, it's in two ways morally preferable.

The same point holds for other examples not involving killing. Consider lying. If you tell a lie, you bring about a bad consequence — that another person has a false belief — by something you do, and intending that consequence as a goal or a means. This is worse than not correcting a false belief she already has because doing so would distract you from something more important. Or consider stealing someone's hat. It produces the result of his not having his hat by action and with intent, which is worse than not retrieving his hat when it's been blown off by the wind and you're busy with something else.

But however powerful they are when they work together, the doing/allowing and intending/foreseeing distinctions can seem less powerful on their own. Is drowning a person in order to get her inheritance worse than not saving her from drowning from the very same motive, and when you could save her easily? In this example, both options intend the person's death as a means; you either drown her or refuse to save her in order to get her inheritance. Does the fact that the first option causes the death rather than merely allowing it make it significantly ethically worse? This does not seem such a compelling claim. Or imagine two actions that both cause death but differ in their motive, one intending death and the other merely foreseeing it. Current medical ethics holds that the first of these actions can be wrong and the second right. These ethics forbid active euthanasia, or giving a patient a lethal injection in order to end his life. But they allow giving a patient a pain-killer that the doctor foresees will, as a side effect, worsen the patient's terminal disease and hasten his death. Though the second action causes death as much as the first, it does so without intending death as a goal or a means. Is this enough to make the second action right? This again seems a less compelling claim. Judeo-Christian morality is on its strongest ground when the doing/allowing and intending/foreseeing distinctions work together, as in the riot and transplant examples. It's more controversial, and has a harder time deciding exactly what to say, when either distinction operates alone.

Like consequentialism, Judeo-Christian morality has distinctive implications about capital punishment. But whereas consequentialism with its single principle tends to make the one issue of deterrence paramount, Judeo-Christian morality with its many principles makes many arguments relevant.

Many versions of Judeo-Christian morality value desert, saying it's good in itself if virtuous actions are rewarded and vicious ones punished. (Consider the importance in Christian thought of rewards and punishments in the afterlife.) If these versions find death an appropriate punishment for the worst crimes such as murder, as many of them do, they can endorse the argument that capital punishment is a demand of justice. Even if this punishment does no more to deter murder than life imprisonment, it's ethically required in itself. (The same conclusion can follow from consequentialist theories that value desert.) Judeo-Christian morality also contains a duty to promote good consequences and prevent bad ones, which means that arguments about deterrence are also relevant. If capital punishment does deter better than life imprisonment, that's a further reason to implement it. But it's not clear which of these two arguments Judeo-Christian morality finds more important. If capital punishment were the deserved punishment for murder but actually encouraged murders, would Judeo-Christian morality still find it right? The answer depends on a question this morality rarely addresses, namely how the value of desert compares to that of happiness and unhappiness. If desert is more important, Judeo-Christian morality will favour capital punishment even at the cost of innocent lives. If that is an unpalatable conclusion, it has to give more weight to preserving happiness. This morality could in principle support the argument that all deliberate killing is wrong, as strict pacifists maintain. But most of its versions prohibit only the killing of the innocent, thereby allowing killing in self-defence and, provided other conditions are met, capital punishment. Judeo-Christian morality also gives some weight to the argument that capital punishment carries the risk of executing an innocent person. It says that each agent, including the state, has a special responsibility to make sure *it* doesn't violate moral duties, and it therefore doesn't count the death of a mistakenly executed person as just one consequence among others, as consequentialism does. But it's again not clear how much weight Judeo-Christian morality gives this argument. A mistakenly executed person dies as a result of something the state does, rather than just of its being inactive. But the state doesn't intend to execute innocent people, either as its goal or a means to its goal. It just foresees that, as an inevitable side effect of a fallible justice system, capital punishment will take some innocent lives. If the doing/allowing distinction is the most important one for Judeo-Christian morality, this fact about capital punishment will be a powerful argument against it. If the intending/foreseeing distinction is more important, the risk of mistaken execution will be less decisive.

The third ethical theory, *libertarianism*, shares some features with Judeo-Christian morality and some with consequentialism. It joins the former in accepting the criticisms that consequentialism both demands and allows too much, but it joins the latter in trying to base all ethical duties on a single fundamental principle or ideal. For libertarianism, the fundamental ideal is liberty or free choice. It holds that everyone has a right to liberty, or, more specifically, a right to the most extensive liberty compatible with the same right to liberty for all. This right has two main aspects.

First, libertarianism holds that each person has a private sphere of action, where what he does directly affects only himself and others who consent to his action, but does not interfere with anyone else's liberty. And it holds that within this private sphere there are no ethical duties or requirements; everything is ethically permitted. If a person has a choice between two options that directly affect only himself, he can't be wrong to choose the one or wrong to choose the other. Within his private life, or when his actions don't interfere with others, he's free or has the right to live as he pleases.

This permissiveness about private choices is very different from what we find in the other two theories. Consequentialism says we have a duty to produce good consequences, not just in others but also in ourselves. If the only good is happiness this may not be a very onerous duty, since most of us already seek our own happiness. But if there are perfectionist goods such as knowledge and achievement, we have a duty to seek these goods whether we want to or not. The same holds for Judeo-Christian morality, many of whose versions contain a duty to develop our talents for goods such as knowledge or achievement, again whether we want to or not. Judeo-Christian morality often contains many other prohibitions of private actions. For example, its traditional Christian versions prohibit suicide, even though that directly affects only the person who takes her life. They also forbid many forms of private sexual activity, such as masturbation and homosexuality. But libertarianism rejects all these views. It says that although people are ethically permitted to develop their talents, they're equally permitted to ignore their talents; that just as people may freely choose to continue living, so they may freely choose to die; and that sexual activities that all participants consent to can't be wrong. They're part of a private sphere where duty has no place and personal liberty is supreme.

Second, libertarianism imposes a duty not to interfere in other people's private spheres, or to prevent them from making the choices they're permitted to make. Our moral freedom extends only so far as others' equal freedom; if we interfere with their legitimate choices, we violate their rights. Thus, if others are permitted to choose between living and dying, we act wrongly if we prevent them from making this choice, as we do if we forcibly kill them. This violates their right to life. If others are permitted to make choices about property they own, we act wrongly if we preempt those choices, for example, by stealing their car. This violates their right to property. The right to liberty granted by libertarianism therefore isn't just a permission. It's a protected permission, which we all have a duty to respect by allowing others to exercise their liberty. Because this duty concerns liberty, however, it isn't violated if a person consents to what we do. Thus we don't violate his right to life if we kill him when he's asked us to, as in voluntary euthanasia. Nor do we violate her property right if we use her car when she's loaned it to us. The general libertarian principle is that we have a right to do whatever doesn't interfere with others' private choices, and what's consented to doesn't interfere with choice.

In applying this principle, libertarianism makes crucial use of the distinction between doing and allowing that figured in Judeo-Christian morality. It holds that you violate another's rights only if his or her liberty is interfered with by something you positively did; there's no violation of rights if you merely fail to prevent a loss of liberty from some other source. Libertarianism therefore agrees with Judeo-Christian morality about the riot example. It would be wrong of you as sheriff to frame and execute an innocent man, since that would involve a positive action that violates his right to life. But you don't violate any rights if you refuse to frame the man and the riot occurs. Though the riot's victims have their liberty interfered with, the interference doesn't come from you and isn't a rights violation on your part. So what you must do as sheriff is not frame the man. In fact, libertarianism goes further with the doing/allowing distinction than Judeo-Christian morality and is therefore an even less demanding ethical theory. It says not only that we needn't make huge sacrifices of our own good to benefit others — as Judeo-Christian morality does — but also that we needn't make any sacrifices at all. If you see someone drowning, and didn't cause them to be drowning, it would be nice and admirable if you saved them, but it isn't a moral duty. If you let them drown, you don't violate their rights and don't act wrongly. Similarly, it would be nice if the rich contributed to famine relief in the developing world, but they don't violate any moral requirement if they keep all their money for themselves. The only moral requirement, according to libertarianism, is the relatively undemanding requirement not to interfere directly with other people's private choices.

Alongside its general right to liberty, libertarianism grants further rights to enforce that right. These rights include a right of self-defence, or a right to use force against those who attempt to violate your rights; a right to exact compensation from those who've harmed you; and a right to threaten and impose punishment on rights-violators. This last right gives libertarianism another distinctive approach to the issue of capital punishment. (See "Is the Death Penalty Cruel and Unusual?", below.)

Libertarianism rejects the argument that all deliberate killing is wrong; it explicitly allows killing in self-defence. It also denies that arguments about desert or deterrence can positively justify capital punishment, in the sense of showing that it's ethically required or something it would be wrong not to impose. The enforcement rights libertarianism grants are, like all rights, only permissions. Though you're permitted to use force in defence against an attack, you're also permitted not to defend yourself but to turn the other cheek if you prefer. Similarly, though a society doesn't act wrongly if it does punish criminals, it also wouldn't act wrongly if it didn't punish, either capitally or at all. But desert and deterrence do play a negative role, because of certain limits on the rights to enforce. Though these rights allow you to take some steps to protect your rights, they don't allow you to take any steps at all. First, your enforcement rights don't allow you to use force that's out of proportion to the threat you're trying to block. In self-defence, you can't kill to stop someone from tickling you or twisting your arm; killing is only allowed against very serious threats. By the same token, capital punishment is only allowed for very serious crimes, perhaps only for murder. Second, your enforcement rights don't allow you to use more force than is necessary to counter the threat. You can't kill in self-defence, even against a threat to your life, if you could save yourself just as well by twisting your attacker's arm or just running away. By the same token, capital punishment is wrong if crimes would be just as effectively deterred by some milder punishment such as life imprisonment. According to libertarianism, capital punishment isn't ruled out in principle; it could be ethically permitted. But it's only permitted for the most serious crimes, and only when it deters those crimes better than less severe punishments. And even when it's permitted, a society that prefers not to use it doesn't do anything wrong.

The three ethical theories I've outlined — consequentialism, Judeo-Christian morality, and libertarianism — disagree about some fundamental ethical issues. If a person is about to make a choice that will harm himself, may we interfere to protect him or must we respect his liberty? Is it worse to cause bad consequences by a positive action than merely to allow bad consequences to happen, or is all that matters ethically the total good or evil that an action will produce? Do we have a duty to make large sacrifices for others, only moderate sacrifices, or no sacrifices at all? And these abstract issues crop up, again and again, in debates about more concrete topics, not just capital punishment but also euthanasia, affirmative action, and many others. On many of these topics, one side thinks the doing/allowing distinction matters while the other does not; on many of them one side focuses on happiness while the other focuses on liberty; and so on. This is where the philosophical approach to ethics can make its greatest contribution. We understand the concrete debates better if we understand the abstract issues on which they so often turn. We also have a better chance of resolving the concrete debates if we approach them philosophically. If we can agree on the abstract issues, however difficult that may be, and if the empirical facts aren't too much in dispute, maybe we can agree on the concrete issues as well.

The essays in this book don't adopt any one of the three ethical theories over the other two. Some discuss the consequences of certain actions and policies; some apply Judeo-Christian ideas; some talk about rights. Nor do the essays often mention the theories explicitly; they don't have space for that. But their unifying aim is to show how the abstract principles that divide the theories are central to debates about concrete issues such as capital punishment, so that deciding about the principles is crucial for resolving the issues. And they try to show how the same principles bear on different issues, so that what look like separate debates have a common underlying structure. This is part of the philosophical approach to ethics: not just stating a position on a concrete issue, or piling up unrelated arguments to support it, but trying to justify it by deriving it from more abstract, more widely applicable, and more explanatory general principles.

Part One

Cultural Identities

*E*ach of us belongs to many groups, and some of those memberships, the important ones, help determine our identity. They've had a pivotal influence on our beliefs and values, and they're also part of our self-identification, or what we value in ourselves. It matters to us to be Canadians, or scientists, or Catholics. The essays to follow examine the nature of these cultural identities and how we should respond to them. Should we treat members of distinct cultures differently, and if so, how and why?

Aboriginal Rights: Do Natives Own the Land?

*C*anada's Native peoples were here first. They lived, hunted, and fished on the land before the arrival of European settlers. Did they therefore own the land, with all the rights that full ownership implies?

If they did, enormous consequences follow. In the parts of Canada where Natives never signed treaties relinquishing the land, it's still rightfully theirs and should be returned to them. At stake here is most of British Columbia. Where they did sign treaties but the negotiators on the other side used fraud or deception, the lands should likewise be returned. At stake here may be much more. After regaining their lands, Natives may have to compensate current owners who in good faith built or paid for improvements on them. But once that compensation is paid, the Natives will rightfully control vast tracts of Canada, including the mineral and other resources they contain.

So did Natives own the land? Western thinking about ownership is heavily influenced by the theories of seventeenth century philosopher John Locke. Locke held that to come to own something not already owned you have to "mix your labour" with it, or work on it in a way that improves it. Consider homesteading on the Canadian prairie. To come to own prairie land, a settler couldn't just claim it or even live on it. He had to work on it, cultivating a certain portion and building a house within three years. He had to make it better before he made it his.

This theory has a certain logic. Before you work the land it's available for everyone to use; if you just use it, you don't separate yourself from anyone else. But if you improve the land, you create value that wasn't there before, and if you own what you create, you own that value. If there's enough land left for others, as there would be on the prairie, the value you create is most of your land's value; by owning it, you own the land.

By this theory's lights, Canada's Natives did own some land before the Europeans arrived. Some Natives, such as the Iroquois of southern Ontario, were farming peoples and owned the land they farmed. Tribes that built permanent villages owned those villages. But the vast majority of land wasn't owned. Where Natives hunted or fished on the land, they used it but didn't improve it; they lived off the land but didn't increase its value. Some tribes were ecologically responsible, assigning hunting rights to particular families so their areas wouldn't be overhunted. But avoiding harming the land isn't the same as improving it. If you have to add value to own, the Natives didn't own much land.

Past Canadian courts used this Lockean theory to deny Natives rights to land. Natives had rights to use the land, the courts ruled, including specifically aboriginal rights to hunt and fish on the land, but no rights to the land itself.

Some philosophers object that this application of the theory applies a foreign standard of value to Natives. Why must the required improvement in the land be agricultural? Wouldn't clearing and ploughing a forest make it worse from a Native point of view? This objection isn't persuasive, because even by Native standards Natives didn't improve the land. They didn't add fish to the rivers or deer to the forests; their use of the land left it as it was.

Despite this, the Lockean argument seems inadequate to Canada's Natives. Something important's left out if we say only that they used the land, as someone might use a field for a touch football game. Canada's Natives, we can say, lived *with* the land, not just on it. They built a way of life in which the land was a central component, and which involved a strong attachment to the land. Surely that attachment gives them some right to the land.

Exactly this argument was made by the Supreme Court of Canada in deciding the Delgamuukw case in 1997. This case involved a claim by the Gitxsan and Wet'suwet'en Native bands to 58 000 sq km in northern British Columbia, an area about the size of Nova Scotia. Their claim had been denied by the courts in British Columbia; they appealed to the Supreme Court; and the Court upheld their appeal, order-ing a new trial or, better still, negotiations about the land.

The Court's decision based the kind of right to land Natives can have, which it called "aboriginal title," in part on just the factors mentioned above: that land a band has occupied for a long time is "integral to the distinctive culture" of the band and the object of a "special bond." Its reasoning went in the opposite direction to Locke's, basing the right to land not on what Natives have done to the land but on what the land has done or meant to them.

At the same time, the Court placed restrictions on the Natives' aboriginal title to land that are not part of simple ownership. Someone who owns land can do virtually anything she wants with it, but aboriginal title, the Court says, allows only those uses that are consistent with the the band's original attachment to the land. A band with title to a river can have an exclusive right to fish it, and even to run whitewater rafting on it even though rafting wasn't part of their ancestors' culture. But the band doesn't have a right to dam the river if that will make it unfishable. Similarly, a band with title to a forest can have an exclusive right to hunt in it and also to practise some logging, but not to strip mine it.

These restrictions make sense given the Court's argument for aboriginal title: if that title stems from the land's place in Native culture, it doesn't allow what will destroy that place. For the same reason, it doesn't allow, as simple ownership does, the sale of the land for profit. And the Court placed another restriction on aboriginal title. It said the Natives' right to land can sometimes be justifiably infringed by the state's interest in economic development, including forestry, mining, and hydroelectric power. In future, Natives have to be consulted about such development and may sometimes have a veto. But their title probably doesn't give them rights where development has already occurred. Where a factory or mine has already been built, it needn't be returned.

The Supreme Court's decision is a wise one. It grants Natives a right to land where the Lockean theory wouldn't, because it focuses not just on what Natives did to the land but on what the land meant for them. It also recognizes that, with that different basis, Native title isn't as far-reaching as traditional ownership. The decision recognizes what's important in the past without creating huge problems for the future.

QUESTIONS FOR DISCUSSION

1. Is it true that you have to improve something that isn't already owned in order to come to own it?

2. Did Canada's Natives have a duty to share the land with the Europeans when the Europeans arrived? If so, how much land? And does it matter whether the Europeans were fleeing famine and other hardships in Europe or just trying out a new locale?

3. Is it true that a special attachment to land based on hunting or fishing can give a group an exclusive right to do other things such as log or extract oil from it? More restrictive reasoning than the Supreme Court's would take Natives' traditional attachment to the land to give them a right only to traditional practices on it. Is this reasoning more consistent than the Court's, or more unfair?

Patriotism: Like Family Love or Racism?

*A*n American once said he regretted having only one life to lose for his country. He was clearly a fan of patriotism. But others call patriotism the last refuge of a scoundrel. Patriotism gets a mixed press, as befits its place in between family love and racism.

All three of these are forms of partiality or favouritism. If you love your family, you care more about their welfare than you do about strangers'. You'll work harder to make them happy and are more upset when they suffer. It's the same with patriotism, which involves caring more about your fellow citizens than about people from other countries. Likewise with racism, where you give preference to those with your skin colour.

Despite this similarity, the forms of partiality differ hugely morally. Family love is admired and even a duty; someone who never favoured his or her children, doing no more for them than for strangers, would be seriously lacking as a parent. But racism is condemned as a horrible evil. Here morality tells us to be colour-blind, showing no preferences based on racial ties. So is patriotism morally like family love or morally like racism?

On the face of it, patriotism looks closer to racism. Your family is a small group that interacts closely. You live together, know each other intimately, and have influenced each other in countless ways. But your race is a huge group, most of whose members you don't know and have never met. In this respect, a nation is like a race. It too is a huge group of people you'll never have contact with.

Seeing this similarity, some philosophers conclude that patriotism, despite its better press, is morally equivalent to racism. If you want your country's trade or immigration to favour people who are now citizens, that's as bad as wanting policies that favour whites as whites. Likewise if, in a war, you want to minimize your country's casualties as against the enemy's. What morality requires is a strict impartiality between people in all countries, your fellow citizens counting no more than people in countries far away.

But this equation of patriotism and racism is too quick, ignoring important differences between patriotism and racism and important similarities between patriotism and family love. Let's look more closely at the latter.

If the interaction among family members gives rise to duties of partiality, it's not just because of its closeness. It's also because of the kind of interaction it is, namely a morally good one. Over the years, family members benefit each other in countless ways: parents raise children, children delight parents, and all work together for the family's common good. The same holds in other relationships that ground duties of partiality, such as those between friends or long-time co-workers. There too the interaction has been not just close but good.

To confirm this, consider a close interaction that's morally evil, such as between guards and prisoners at a Nazi labour camp. Do the prisoners have a duty to care specially about the guards, because of what they've done together? Not if what they've done is evil. Or consider two guards at the camp. Does their shared history of terrorizing inmates mean they should favour each other's interests? Again, not if the history is evil.

So there are two things about family members that justify their special mutual concern: the closeness of their interaction and the good that interaction has done. The first of these isn't present among fellow citizens of a country, but the second is.

Your fellow citizens are people you've worked together with to produce the benefits of a stable society. You've voted for or otherwise supported governments that have ensured the rule of law, economic redistribution, and the other conditions for prosperity and well-being. Your country may also have done good internationally, say, through peace keeping. Though your interactions with your fellow citizens haven't been close they've been productive, because they've run through powerful state institutions.

This isn't true of your relations with members of your race, which has no institutions. The whites and blacks of the world are spread across it, with no organization through which they can work together. By supporting the Canadian government, Canadians have done important things together; the same isn't true of any race.

It doesn't follow that Canadians should care as much about their fellow citizens as about their families. Though your country shares one feature with your family, it doesn't share another. If that other feature — closeness of interaction — also matters, then the degree of partiality that's justified is less. And that seems right. Not even the most ardent patriot thinks he should care as much about his fellow-citizens as about his children.

There are other limits on the degree of patriotism that's justified. If the key is a shared history that's good, then no partiality is justified when the relevant history is evil. Consider Germans right after the Second World War. Given what they had just done together — launching an aggressive war, practising genocide — there was no ground at all for patriotism or national partiality. Today, after 50 years of responsible international behaviour, Germans can perhaps feel some pride in themselves as a country. But they couldn't right after the Holocaust.

In addition, any justified partiality is limited by other moral duties, including those granting rights to all persons. So even when you favour your fellow citizens, you can't do this in a way that violates others' rights. This is true of family love as well. The mother in Texas who tried to kill her daughter's schoolmate so the daughter could win a cheerleading contest was expressing her love in a way that isn't right. Similarly a nation, even one that justifiably prefers its own citizens' interests, can't do so by starting wars or abusing foreigners' rights.

Morality doesn't always require you to treat everyone equally; you can sometimes have preferences. This is clearest in the family, but it's also true to a degree in your country. Caring more about your fellow citizens isn't justified to the same degree as caring more about your children, but it's not like a racist preference for whites as whites. Patriotism may not always be worth dying for, but it's also not always a trait of scoundrels.

QUESTIONS FOR DISCUSSION

1. Do Canadians feel as much patriotism as they should? If not, in what ways should they

express patriotism? And what should be the basis of their patriotism?

2. Is it true that the basis of your special concern for your family or country is something about your history, that is, about the past? Or do other factors play a role?

3. Is favouritism toward members of your race always morally wrong? Even if it's wrong for members of a dominant race such as whites to prefer each other's interests, is this also wrong for members of persecuted races, such as Jews and blacks, at least so long as the persecution continues?

Canadian Nationalism and the Distinctiveness Fetish

*C*anadians care about medicare; it's a source of national pride and central to our attachment to Canada. Some Canadians care especially about medicare because they think it's distinctive of Canada, at least as compared with the United States. But it's an odd idea: that we should care most about what's distinctively Canadian, as so many discussions of Canadian nationalism assume. Would medicare matter less if the United States had it too?

It isn't hard to imagine. John F. Kennedy might not have been assassinated in 1963; Hubert Humphrey might have been elected president in 1968. Either might have instituted full medicare in the United States. If he had, our own medicare would be less distinctive. To think Canadian nationalism must focus on what's distinctively Canadian is to think Canadian medicare would then be less important. But that's to misunderstand the basis of healthy national feelings.

Nationalism is a form of partiality, of caring more about some people than about others. A

Canadian nationalist cares more about relieving poverty among her fellow Canadians than among foreigners; she wants immigration policy decided mainly by its effects on people now in Canada. In this respect nationalism is like other forms of partiality, such as caring more about your spouse or children than about strangers, and can be understood by analogy with them.

If you care specially about your spouse, it's partly for some of their qualities: their intelligence, trustworthiness, and so on. But you know these qualities aren't unique. Other people have them, some even to a higher degree. What attaches you specially to your spouse is something that isn't a quality in the normal sense. It's their having participated with you in a shared history. No one else, no matter how intelligent or trustworthy, could be the very person you fell in love with that summer, who helped you through that depression, and who did all those other things with you.

Nationalism has a similar basis. A Canadian nationalist thinks Canada has good qualities, like a commitment to tolerance and equality. But she needn't think Canada is the best country in the world. What ties her specially to her fellow-Canadians is something historical: that they grew up with her here, experiencing the same weather and TV shows, electing and then despising the same politicians.

That's why it wouldn't matter if the United States too had medicare. Canadian medicare would still be a good thing about Canada, and it would still be part of our history. It would be something we developed, from Tommy Douglas and Emmett Hall through the Canada Health Act. It would be something we've all participated in, both as users of medicare and as contributors to it. American medicare might be similar, but it wouldn't be the system we've lived with here.

So it's a mistake to tie Canadian nationalism to distinctively Canadian qualities. And it isn't a harmless mistake. It's had several destructive effects on Canadian national life.

First, it's led many Canadians to embrace false beliefs about their country. It's often said that Canada is, distinctively, a country of diverse regions, not just Quebec compared to English Canada but every province compared to the others. But do we really believe that, say, Nova Scotia is more different from Alberta than Scotland is from England, or than northern India is from southern India? Reverting to medicare, do we think we're the only country in the world with social programs?

Some nationalists recognize that in the world as a whole, Canada is a fairly average industrial democracy. But they say the point isn't to be distinctive in the world. It's to be distinctive in North America, to be an egalitarian or sharing society in the same region as the United States. That's because the United States isn't just another country. It's our immensely powerful neighbour and the source of our constant existential question: why aren't we part of them? Only as distinct from the behemoth to the south does Canada have a reason to exist.

But there's no such existential question. Canadians have no interest in joining the United States, as they show repeatedly in opinion polls. And it's not because of any bogus ideas about distinctiveness. (They root for Canadian sprinters at the Olympics without wondering whether they sprint in a distinctively Canadian way.) Think again about your spouse and children. Do you face a constant question about whether to join the family next door, just because they have a bigger house or more money? Of course not. You're attached to your family by a history your neighbours don't share, and that's attachment enough.

Second, the distinctiveness fetish has corrupted Canadian politics, offering an all-purpose counter to any proposal: "That will lead to the Americanization of Canada." This counter is used by the left to oppose privatization and deficit-cutting, and by the right to oppose employment equity and the Charter of Rights. But if something American is bad, it has to be bad for some reason other than that it's American. So let's hear that other reason. And may some American things not be good?

Or consider Prime Minister Jean Chrétien's remark that Canada without Quebec is unthinkable. It assumes that Canada is thinkable only if it's distinct from the United States., and will be less distinct without Quebec. But the assumption, again, is false. Canada without Quebec would be a smaller Canada; it would lack, tragically, many people who participated in our history. But it would have no more reason to break up than a family would after one member runs away.

Also corrupted is commentary on the arts, which often assumes the main point of Canadian art is to express what's distinctively Canadian. This view is hard to apply to arts like music. How does a classical violinist play Beethoven in a distinctively Canadian way? And it's even constricting when applied to literature. There are uniquely Canadian experiences, and literature that captures them can be as great as any literature anywhere. But there are also universal experiences, such as falling in love, aging, and dying. Writing and exploring those experiences can likewise be great; if it's by a Canadian, that makes it ours.

Canadian nationalism hasn't always been based on ideas about distinctiveness. Think of the nationalism of the years following the Second World War, based on Canada's participation in that war. Canadians of the late 1940s didn't think they had fought in a war no one else had fought, or even fought in a distinctive way. It was enough that they

— people with a common history — had fought alongside other nations and fought well.

This older nationalism was healthier than any current version based on distinctiveness. To care that your nation's good qualities be distinctive is to care both that your nation have them and that other nations do not. (The second, by the logic of distinctiveness, is just as important as the first.) But isn't it nasty to want other nations not to share your own's good qualities. Isn't it a kind of malice?

Distinctiveness nationalists should ask themselves whether they aren't prone to this malice. Do they take a kind of comfort from the violence and inequality of the United States, just because they make Canada different? Are they partly pleased when Newt Gingrich and Pat Buchanan have political successes in the United States, because they wouldn't have them here? If so, their ill-wishing only works through the nasty logic of distinctiveness.

Canadian nationalism needn't be nasty. We can, while recognizing Canada's weaknesses, treasure its good qualities and hope other nations share them. We can want all nations to respect human rights and practise tolerance; we can hope the United States one day becomes less violent and even institutes medicare. If it does, Canada will be less distinctive. But that won't matter to Canadians freed of fraudulent ideas about distinctiveness and attached to each other, as to their families, by the solid bond of a common history.

QUESTIONS FOR DISCUSSION

1. Is a shared history enough to ground feelings of special attachment to a group of people such as a family or nation, or is more required?

2. How true is it that caring about good things that are distinctive about your nation involves wanting other nations not to have those good things? How often does an interest in distinctiveness involve malice?

3. Would the world be a better place if it contained many different and distinct cultures than if all became the same through globalization? Why or why not?

Why Study Different Cultures?

At my high school 30 years ago we really learned about Britain. In Grades 9 and 10 the only history we did was British history, which we studied chronologically, for two years, from the Roman conquest in 55 B.C. to 1900. In the same grades the only literature we did was British literature, which we again studied chronologically, from *Beowulf* in the Dark Ages to 1900. For two years it was Britain, Britain, Britain.

One reason for this curriculum was the belief that Canada was an essentially British nation. We were a former British colony; we had British institutions and the Queen was our head of state. To study Britain, it was thought, was really to study ourselves. A second was the belief that British culture was the best culture. It had the most important history and the most profound literature; to study it was also to study the best.

No school today would focus so exclusively on Britain. Instead, the current trend is to a multicultural curriculum, one that teaches about the many cultures both within Canada and elsewhere in the world. What's taught is less a single culture than the diversity of cultures and of ways that people live.

This multicultural approach to education is welcome. But though there are good reasons for it, there are also some bad ones. And there was something valuable in that two years' concentration on Britain that it would be a shame to lose.

One good reason for the new curriculum is a changed understanding of Canada. In the 1960s, Canada was already ceasing to be a primarily British nation, and it's nothing like that now. A full understanding of its history must look at the contributions not only of French Canadians (whom we did study 30 years ago), but also of Native Canadians and immigrants (whom we didn't). More specifically, it must see Canada's present character as resulting from the interactions of all these groups, with of course influences from other countries.

This argument for multiculturalism still assumes, as my school did 30 years ago, that we have special reason to study our own nation. And this is a valid assumption. Our lives will be far more affected by our Canadian fellow citizens and government than by foreigners; that makes the history behind them more important for us to learn. Likewise, Canadian literature is closer to the problems of our lives. Finally, importance aside, we legitimately can and should care more about our own culture, just because it's ours. That's patriotism, favouring your own nation because it's the one in which you were raised.

A second reason for the new curriculum is an increased confidence in Canada. Thirty years ago there wasn't much Canadian fiction or poetry that educators thought ranked with the best of British literature. That's no longer so. Canada may not have produced a Shakespeare — how many cultures have? — but there's lots of Canadian writing that meets high international standards. Studying ourselves is consistent with studying the best.

This argument still assumes, as my school did, that we should study what meets objective standards of quality. And the same assumption justifies teaching more about foreign and especially non-Western cultures. Not only is British culture not the single best, neither is Western European culture. There are many great works from other continents. For this reason, many universities are replacing History of Western Civilization courses with ones that include materials from distant cultures such as China and India.

There's another reason for studying distant cultures. We may think some practice of ours is unavoidable and follows from universal human nature; if we learn that it's not shared by other cultures, we can see it as just one option among many. Alternatively, if we learn that what we do is also done in other cultures, we can see that our practice doesn't have distinctively Canadian causes. It probably developed here for the same reasons it developed everywhere. Either way, understanding other cultures can diminish our arrogance about our own.

These are all good reasons for a multicultural curriculum. But though they reach a different conclusion than my British-loving high school, they start from the same assumptions: that we should study both our own culture and what's best. The bad reasons for multiculturalism abandon these assumptions.

One of them denies that there's any such thing as objective quality in cultures. Not only is the claim that British culture is best unfounded, but any such claim is just a naked grab for power. It's what the powerful use to impose their values on the weak and has no objective merit. And if no culture can be superior, we should study all cultures equally.

This "postmodern" argument is an over-reaction to the facts. That some claims to cultural superiority have been arrogant and unfounded doesn't mean that all must be. We should only make these claims cautiously and after a great deal of study, study that may reveal richness in other cultures we hadn't suspected. But the study may also reveal that, in the end, some cultures are higher. Within our culture, Shakespeare is an undeniably greater writer than Stephen King, and, however hard it may be to determine, there's no reason why the same can't hold across cultures.

What's more, the postmodern argument is, like all relativist arguments, self-defeating. If all claims of superiority are unfounded, then what about the claimed superiority of a multicultural curriculum? Aren't its proponents, when they criticize an exclusively British curriculum, likewise making only a naked grab for power? If they aren't, can't there be objective superiority for some curricula and cultures?

A second bad reason for multiculturalism says it's needed to show respect for other cultures and their members. If we give more attention to one culture, it's said, we imply that other cultures are less worthy and also undermine the self-esteem of students from them. If those students are to feel valued, and to make the best of their abilities, the curriculum must pay attention to their cultures too.

This argument assumes that the only reason to favour studying a culture is that it's best, but that's not so. We can prefer studying Canadian culture because it's ours and with no implication that it's better than other cultures. And this preference need have no improper effects on students' self-esteem. If the Canadian curriculum left out the contributions of Natives and French Canadians, they would feel rightly aggrieved; their cultures have been essential parts of Canada, and they're slighted if those cultures are ignored. The same is true of immigrants as a group. But it's not true of particular immigrant groups, such as the Irish or Chinese. Their ancestors chose to come to Canada; they chose to enter our culture. Whatever their cultures' objective merits, they're not essential to the Canadian culture we rightfully focus on.

So we shouldn't supplement the good reasons for a multicultural curriculum with bad ones, and in particular shouldn't make that curriculum more multicultural than the good reasons warrant. And there's another reason to restrain our multiculturalism.

For all its narrowness, my Grades 9 and 10 curriculum did have an impressive unity. Because we studied only works of British literature, we could study them in context, seeing how they compared to earlier works in the same tradition. It was the same with the history; when we studied one century of British politics we could see how it related to previous centuries'. We could also relate the literature to the history. When we read a play of the seventeenth century, we knew what was happening socially and politically when the play was written.

This is a unity we should want in any curriculum. When it's present, the more a student studies in a given area the more he can learn from studying more, because the earlier material puts him in a position to see more deeply into what comes later. To borrow language from economics, this unity allows "increasing returns from scale," where the more you've put into something the more you get from further effort on it.

There's a danger that a multicultural curriculum can lose this unity. It can become a smorgasbord, with a little about Native Canadians, a little about Britain, a little India, China, and so on. Students learn a little about many cultures but not a lot about any one and therefore not a lot about anything. They have a broad acquaintance with cultures but no deep understanding of what any culture is.

This poses a difficult challenge to educators today: how to balance the good reasons for multiculturalism with the desirability of a unified curriculum. How do we expose students to many cultures while allowing them to fully explore one? How do we keep them both from narrowness and from dilettantism? There's certainly been progress since the time when studying culture in Canadian schools meant studying only Britain, but we don't want that progress to go with a loss of depth in what our students learn.

QUESTIONS FOR DISCUSSION

1. How much should the curriculum at Canadian high schools and universities focus on Canada, and how much on foreign cultures? What should the balance between Canadian and non-Canadian content be?

2. What can we learn from studying distant cultures such as India and China, or ancient cultures such as Greece and Rome? Are these cultures relevant to Canada today, or is studying them a waste of time?

3. How should a school or university show respect for the many cultures present in Canada today?

Should Whites Write about Minorities?

*I*n 1988, the Toronto-based Women's Press split over a demand by women of colour on its collective that the press not publish stories by white women about black women's experience. The next year, *Where the Spirit Lives* and *Bonebird*, a film and novel by whites but involving Native characters, were condemned by some Natives as "racist." The issue is still hotly debated: should white artists create works about characters from racial minorities?

Three arguments have been given why not. One is that whites don't understand the experience of racial minorities and will therefore misrepresent it. A second is that whites' treatment of minority subjects makes it harder for minority artists to find audiences. If a white film-maker gets funding for a film about Natives, this makes it harder for a Native film-maker to get funding. Finally, white treatment of minority subjects involves "appropriation": the theft of stories and forms from the cultures and artists to whom they belong.

These arguments are related. All assume a social context where racial minorities aren't equal participants in Canadian society and their artists are not equally heard. Outside this context, none of the arguments would be made.

Imagine that Canada had a flourishing community of Native artists whose works were widely appreciated. If a white novel misdescribed Native experience, it would be quickly recognized as doing so. And such a novel would be unlikely. White writers as well as readers would be educated by the strong presence of Native culture around them.

But this isn't our situation. Natives in Canada are marginalized, isolated on reserves or scattered in cities. Their cultural voices aren't heard in the mainstream. If a white treats a Native subject, he or she is likely to get it wrong and, worse, to be taken by whites as getting it right.

This isn't the grand claim that it is in principle impossible for a non-Native to understand Native culture. It's the realistic claim that, in current conditions, this understanding is very difficult.

Social context is equally vital to the other arguments. White works wouldn't keep Native artists from a wider audience if Natives already had that audience. Nor would there be "appropriation" if Natives were succeeding in telling their stories in their own way.

The argument about appropriation takes the idea of stealing audiences further. Imagine that a white writes a novel that distorts Native symbols. White readers will come to understand the symbols in a distorted way, making it harder for a Native to reach them with authentic art. (Think what Native artists must already struggle against in the stereotypes created by Hollywood.) And there's a greater danger. If the white's novel is read by Natives, they too may understand the symbols inauthentically. The Native artist then can't speak even to his or her own people. Finally, even if white works on minority themes do no harm, it is galling for minority artists who can't get published to see others' books about their people so widely read. It graphically underlines their artistic marginalization.

Read in their social context, these arguments urge respect and consideration for minority cultures struggling to establish or preserve themselves. The thought should be familiar to Canadians.

In the 1960s, our artists fought for and won Canadian content restrictions on radio and television. Some who opposed free trade with the United States in 1988 did so partly for fear that it threatened these cultural protections.

These stands recognized that a minority culture — this time Canadian culture in the broader context of North America — can be vulnerable and need help to develop itself. Can we not extend the same help to our minorities?

The response of Canadian artists to the issue of "voice" has been unsettling. Some, predictably, have raised the spectre of censorship. But this is a red herring. No one is proposing laws against white novels about Natives or even formal changes in the policies of arts councils. You can think something is undesirable without thinking anyone should be forcibly prevented from doing it.

But doesn't talk of what artists shouldn't write create a climate favourable to censorship? At best this is a pink herring. White writers are being urged to be socially responsible in their choice and handling of subjects. If asking artists to be responsible creates a climate for censorship, we've lived in that climate for decades.

Others ask, "Where do you draw the line? Are Natives not to write about whites, or white city-dwellers about white farmers?" The question answers itself. Since the arguments for restraint assume the unequal status of minority cultures, they apply only to works about minorities.

There's no reason why blacks shouldn't write about whites, or whites about each other. There's even no reason why, in some egalitarian future, whites shouldn't write about Natives.

Canadians more than anyone should under- stand that a minority within a larger majority can contain minorities within itself. We should listen sympathetically when minorities ask us for what we have won for ourselves.

QUESTIONS FOR DISCUSSION

1. Does it make sense to talk of cultural "appro- priation," as if stories and symbols are owned by the people who first used them?

2. How much should artists strive to be truthful — which means writing about what they know best — and how much should they try to stretch their and their readers' imaginations?

3. If Canadians don't as individuals want to buy works by Native or Canadian artists, why should government regulations favour those artists?

Philosophy, Morality, and The English Patient

*T*he movie *The English Patient*, based on the novel by Michael Ondaatje, won nine Academy Awards in 1997, including for Best Picture. This last award normally goes only to serious movies, ones that address important themes. But looked at this way, *The English Patient* is a disturbing choice. It has a moral perspective on the events it describes, but it is a me-centred and immoral one. Philosophy can help explain why.

In saying this I don't assume that all art is subject to moral critique, a common view in the nineteenth century. People then believed that even landscape painting and instrumental music have as their main function to morally improve their audience, and should be evaluated for how well they do so. I think it's obvious that many works of art have no moral content, so a moral commentary on them is irrelevant. But other works, especially of literature and drama, raise and explore moral issues. And when they do, we can ask how well they do so.

The English Patient has a moral issue at the centre of its plot. In an Italian villa at the end of the

Second World War, a burn victim is slowly dying. His face is scarred beyond recognition and he claims not to know his own identity. But one character, Caravaggio, has figured out who the patient is. He is Count Laszlo de Almasy, a Hungarian desert explorer who just before the war gave the German army crucial desert maps that enabled them to attack Tobruk and almost win the war in North Africa. Caravaggio himself was captured and tortured in that offensive. He thinks Almasy is guilty of betrayal about the maps and wants to bring him to account. Caravaggio has killed everyone else responsible for his capture and torture, and he now wants to kill Almasy.

So a key question is: did Almasy act wrongly in handing over the maps? The rest of the movie addresses this question by showing what led to Almasy's choice.

Before the war, Almasy was deeply in love with a married woman, Katherine Clifton. Much of the movie describes their passionate and all-consuming affair. But just before the war, Katherine was seriously injured in a desert plane crash that also killed her husband. Almasy, who was present, carried her to shelter in a cave and promised to return with help. His first attempt to get that help, from the British army, was rebuffed. Confronted by someone with no identification papers and a foreign accent, they instead arrested him as a spy. After escaping from the British, Almasy went to the German army. But to get their help he needed to offer them something in return. As the only way to keep his promise to Katherine, and from profound love for her, he gave the Germans the maps.

When he hears this story, Caravaggio says he no longer has any desire to punish Almasy. The "poison," he says, has left him. And the movie's treatment of Almasy is now overwhelmingly sympathetic. Its emotional high point comes when Almasy, finding he has returned to Katherine too late, emerges from the cave carrying her dead body. Tears stream down his face; the photography is lush and gorgeous; the background music swells. As portrayed here, Almasy is an entirely romantic figure. There is an equally sympathetic treatment as Almasy, having requested a morphine overdose, dies at the movie's end. Again both the camera and his nurse surround him with unqualified love.

After his escape from the British, Almasy faced a choice between a political end, resisting Nazism or at least not colluding with it, and a personal end, keeping his promise to Katherine. And the movie's treatment implies that his preference for the personal end was understandable and even right. This is implicit in the movie's most important line, a remark of Katherine's that it emphasizes by repeating: "Betrayals in war are childlike compared to our betrayals in peace." Loyalty in love, this line says, is more important than loyalty to political ends such as those fought for in war. Whatever its consequences for politics, any action done from love is right.

It is this utter denigration of the political that makes *The English Patient* immoral. There was not just some political end at stake in the Second World War; there was resistance to Nazism, a movement threatening millions of innocent people. Yet the movie treats even this end as morally inconsequential. Its attitude is therefore the opposite of that taken in *Casablanca*, a movie likewise set in North Africa in the Second World War. In *Casablanca*, Humphrey Bogart's character Rick sacrifices his love for Ilsa in order to join the fight against Nazism. As he tells her and her husband, "The problems of three little people don't amount to a hill of beans in this crazy world." In *The English Patient*, by contrast, the fight against Nazism is blithely sacrificed for love. The problems of the world, the movie says, and of the millions of people threatened by Nazism don't amount to a hill of beans beside those of two love-crazed people.

This critique of *The English Patient* is most compelling given a certain assumption about its plot: that given the time it took Almasy to reach the British army, escape from them, and reach the Germans, he should have known there was no chance Katherine would be alive when he reached the cave. He was keeping a promise to someone dead, and however romantic that may be it has little moral weight beside a duty not to collude with Nazism.

This assumption may be challenged, however. Maybe Almasy got to the Germans fast enough that he did have a reasonable chance of saving Katherine. Then his choice was fraught in a way that Rick's in *Casablanca* is not. Whatever Rick does, he knows Ilsa will be safe. But for Almasy, to honour the political demand is to consign his loved one to death. Given this circumstance, is his choice so obviously wrong?

The English Patient, revealingly, doesn't bother to settle this morally crucial detail of plot. But let's grant that Katherine might still have been alive. A movie could then portray Almasy as caught between two powerful but conflicting moral demands, one personal and one political, with some horrible violation inevitable whichever choice he makes. If he resists Nazism he fails the woman he loves; if he saves her he colludes with moral evil. This possible movie has the structure some find in classical Greek tragedies such as Aeschylus's *Agamemnon*, where the protagonist faces a tragic conflict between two competing moral duties and cannot avoid doing something morally wrong. Whichever duty he chooses, he is guilty of violating the other and must pay for that guilt. But this possible movie is not *The English Patient*, which gives Almasy's political duty no serious attention at all. When love is at stake, its demands not only outweigh the competing demands of politics but render them trivial.

This is certainly Almasy's view. Before the war he thought the coming conflict was just one between silly nationalisms. In the Italian villa, after his story has been told, he thinks his choice about the maps was not just right but obviously so. Told that his explorer friend Madox killed himself when he learned of Almasy's betrayal, he is simply and entirely surprised: why would anyone react like that? And he offers excuses for his choice that are morally pathetic. One is that his action did not mean that any extra people were killed; it only changed which people were killed. But even if this is true (and how does Almasy know it?), he couldn't have known it at the time. His transfer of the maps could easily have led to a Nazi victory in North Africa, with incalculable effects on the future course of the war. And doesn't it matter whether the people killed in war are guilty Nazi aggressors or morally innocent defenders?

Almasy's view is also the movie's. As I have said, its treatment of him, especially in its most emotionally loaded scenes, is entirely sympathetic. And this sympathy is almost inevitable, given the way the movie frames the moral issue Almasy faces.

In a recent moral defence of the movie, Ondaatje has borrowed from that central line of Katherine's. Its theme, he says, is "love, desire, betrayals in war, and betrayals in peace." This is indeed how the movie presents Almasy's choice, as one between conflicting loyalties and different possible betrayals. But the concepts of loyalty and betrayal are essentially personalized, or me-centred. I can be loyal to a person *I* love or to the nation *I* belong to or to a group of people specially connected to *me*. But I can't be loyal to a stranger, and I can't betray a stranger. In framing the moral issue as it does, therefore, the movie frames it in an essentially me-centred way. Almasy is to ask himself which of the people specially connected to him he should care most about, or which attachment to him, that of his lover or of his nation, is morally most important.

But this approach entirely ignores a more impersonal type of moral demand. This demand is impersonal not in the sense that it is not about people but in that it is about people independently of any special connection to oneself, or just as human beings. Other people matter morally in themselves and we have duties to care about them whatever their relation to us. This impersonal type of duty was utterly central in the Second World War. Nazism threatened the lives of millions of innocent people and regardless of their nationality, those people needed protection. This is clearly recognized in *Casablanca*. In that movie, Rick has no reason of loyalty to join the fight against Nazism; he is an American and the United States is not yet in the war. But he sees that, loyalties aside, Nazism is an evil that must be resisted. His reason for fighting is therefore not me-centred but, in the sense I am using, impersonal. And this kind of reason is given no place in *The English Patient*. By recognizing only the concepts of loyalty and betrayal, that movie leaves no room for a demand to care about people only as people.

That is why the movie inevitably sympathizes with Almasy's choice. If the alternatives are loyalty to a particular person one loves and loyalty to something as abstract as a nation, of course the former is more important. It's the same with E.M. Forster's famous remark that if he had to choose between betraying his country and betraying his friend, he hoped he would have the guts to betray his country. As described, that choice again seems correct. But in each case this is only because the choice is described in a tendentiously incomplete way, one leaving out impersonal considerations. And those considerations are often morally decisive. Consider: if you had to choose between betraying your friend and colluding in the murder of millions of innocent people, would you hope you had the guts to murder those people?

This is the central immorality of *The English Patient*: its reduction of all moral demands to me-centred demands, ones based on other people's relationships to oneself. The reduction appears in many places in the movie.

One is its taking seriously another of Almasy's pathetic excuses. He wasn't guilty of betrayal in handing over the maps, he says, because the British betrayed him first in refusing him help to save Katherine. Set aside the question of whether the British really did treat Almasy at all badly. He was in disputed territory on the brink of war with no papers; he was abusive in his manners and gave no satisfactory explanation for his request. But that aside, why should one little betrayal by the British license him to collude with Nazis? That conclusion would only follow if the coming war were, as Almasy thought, just another conflict between silly nationalisms. But of course in this war one side, whatever the other's failings, was incomparably morally worse. That is why Elizabeth Pathy Salett was entirely correct to say, in the *Washington Post* article to which Ondaatje responded, that the movie's "presentation of a moral equivalency between the Germans and Allies trivializes the significance of the choices men like Almasy made."

Even the voice against Almasy in the movie speaks in me-centred terms. That voice is Caravaggio, and what does Caravaggio want? He above all wants revenge, and revenge is again a personalized concept. I can want revenge only for a wrong done to me or someone closely connected to me, and I get revenge only if I inflict it myself. In both respects a desire for revenge contrasts with a desire for justice, which can be aroused by wrongdoing against anyone and can be satisfied when punishment is imposed by anyone, including the impersonal state. But expressing the moral challenge to Almasy in terms of revenge again has a trivializing effect. It reduces that challenge to a "poison" that can be easily extracted when Almasy's story is told. And it utterly underdescribes the subject of that challenge. As part of his torture, Caravaggio had his thumbs cut off. This means that he can no longer do sleight of hand tricks — when he tries one with an egg he drops it — and can no longer ply his former trade as a pickpocket. It is hard to think of a less adequate representation of the threat posed by Nazism.

There are, then, three levels of moral critique of *The English Patient*. First, the movie sympathizes with a choice that is simply morally wrong. Second, it sees nothing at all problematic about a choice that, even if not simply wrong, violates an important political duty. Third, the movie casts its moral considerations entirely in the me-centred terms of loyalty and betrayal, never recognizing the impersonal demands that were so central in its setting of the Second World War. Of these critiques, the second and especially the third are philosophical. Moral philosophy doesn't consider completely different issues from ordinary moral thought. It considers the same issues but at a higher level of abstraction, identifying the principles and structures of principles that underlie and explain particular moral judgements. In this as in many cases, it is the most philosophical critique that is most important. It is because it recognizes only me-centred and no impersonal moral duties that *The English Patient* sees nothing troubling in, and even sympathizes with, a highly questionable choice. *Casablanca* was very much a product of its time. Its impersonal moral vision expresses the experience of people who were fighting to resist aggression on another continent. *The English Patient* is, unfortunately, also a product of its time, one in which many people have abandoned concern for those in other countries or even for less fortunate members of their own society. It is a time of withdrawal from the impersonal concerns of politics into a smaller realm focussed on the self and its few chosen intimates. It is no surprise that *The English Patient* won its Academy Awards. The movie has the kind of high-minded tone that Academy voters find impressive. And its substance fits the depressing tenor of our time.

QUESTIONS FOR DISCUSSION

1. Is it appropriate to evaluate films and other works of art in moral terms, or is art a realm separate from morality?

2. Which is ethically more important, loyalty to particular people such as your family and friends or loyalty to your nation? How does either compare in ethical importance to the demands imposed by the needs of people just as people, that is, of strangers or people in distant nations?

3. In what ways are the concepts of loyalty and betrayal me-centred, and in what ways are they not? If we act from feelings of loyalty, are we acting selfishly?

Part Two

Biomedical Ethics

*B*iomedical ethics discusses what is
right and wrong in medicine and health
care. The essays in this part deal
especially with issues about life and
death, both at the beginning of life —
abortion, surrogate motherhood, genetic
engineering — and at its end —
euthanasia. Many of these issues arise
from developments in medical technology.
Technology now allows us to determine
when and what kinds of humans are
born, and when humans die. Is it right or
wrong for us to make these choices?

Abortion and the Moral Standing of the Fetus

*A*s in other countries, the abortion debate continues to rage in Canada. But it still generates little light, marked as it is by dishonesty on one side and arrogance on the other.

The central issue in the abortion debate is what philosophers call the "moral standing" of the fetus. Does the fetus have the same moral standing as an adult, so is it wrong to kill it whenever it would be wrong to kill an adult? Or does it have less or no standing?

Pro-choice presentations are dishonest because they don't state or properly argue for a position on this issue. They concentrate on the right of the woman to control her body or to exercise reproductive freedom.

All can agree that women have these rights, but like others, they are limited by any stronger rights in other beings with standing. If abortion involves killing a fetus, and a fetus has full moral standing, its right to life outweighs any rights of the woman.

Equally dishonest is the argument that abortion, though a difficult issue, is one each woman must decide on her own. This would be reasonable if abortion involved only a woman herself. But if it affects another being with standing, especially if it kills that being, it is just the kind of act our laws should prohibit.

The pro-life side doesn't ignore the issue of the fetus's standing. On the contrary, it makes it the centrepiece of its position. But it is arrogant in assuming this is a simple issue to which it has the simple solution.

Most pro-lifers aren't vegetarians. They don't think it always wrong to kill an animal, and wouldn't hesitate to do so to protect an adult human from even moderate harm. Like most of us, they think adult humans have greater moral standing than animals.

Why do adult humans have greater standing than animals? It can't just be because they're humans. That would be "speciesism," like saying whites count more than Orientals because they're whites. If humans have more standing than animals, they must have special properties that give them this standing.

Secular moralists agree what sort of properties these are. Some cite rationality, some uniquely rich enjoyments, some free choice, but all base adult humans' greater standing in some aspect of their unique mental life.

This is relevant to the abortion debate. The simplest way to argue that fetuses have the same standing as adults is to say they actually have the properties that give adults that standing. But fetuses don't yet have rationality or rich enjoyments. If we look at their actual properties, these seem morally indistinguishable from animals'.

In his challenge to Canada's old abortion law, Joe Borowski based his argument on the fetus's actual properties. His witnesses testified, for example, that a fetus produces its own blood and moves away from a needle. But animals too produce blood and avoid needles. How can you show that a fetus has more standing than animals by pointing to properties it shares with animals?

The alternative is to argue for the fetus's standing on the basis of its potential. The fetus doesn't now have rationality or rich enjoyments, but unlike any animal, it has the potential to develop into a being that does.

This argument also has difficulties. If the fetus has the potential for special properties, why doesn't this give it just the potential for standing, rather than actual standing now? And if the fetus has the potential to develop into a being with a mental life, isn't the same true of an unfertilized sperm and egg? Yet does anyone think contraception is morally equivalent to murder?

The pro-life argument faces a dilemma. If we look at the fetus's actual properties, it seems morally indistinguishable from animals. If we look at its potential, it seems indistinguishable from unfertilized cells.

This dilemma may be partly avoidable. There may be different meanings of "potential," so a 28-week fetus has the potential for mental life in a more significant sense than unfertilized cells, one that confers moral standing where the other doesn't. On reflection, this has to be so. A 2-week-old baby doesn't, any more than a fetus, actually have rationality or rich enjoyments. Yet only an extreme view thinks it in principle permissible to kill babies. If babies have full standing this must rest on their potential, which must differ from that of mere cells.

This seems the one route to a defensible view about the fetus. But if there are two kinds of potential, one conferring standing while the other doesn't, when does the first, more significant, potential appear?

The answer depends on what defines the first potential, which is a difficult philosophical (not medical) issue. But it is unlikely to appear at conception. The relevant potential is for a rich mental life, and differs from the potential of cells. This suggests that it requires the actual presence of the brain structures that will later ground a mental life. These brain structures develop during the second trimester of pregnancy, but are not present before.

We seem led, then, to a moderate position on abortion, one permitting it early in pregnancy but not later on. When the Canadian government proposed legislation reflecting this position, its draft was attacked as a cynical compromise between two principled views. This assumes that to be principled, moral beliefs must be simple, which is false. If we think seriously about abortion, without dishonestly ignoring the fetus or arrogantly assuming its standing, we may be led to a principled justification of the politically most acceptable view.

QUESTIONS FOR DISCUSSION

1. Why is it relevant to ask whether those who oppose abortion are vegetarians?

2. Does it make more sense to determine the fetus's standing by looking at the properties it actually has or at its potential?

3. Even if the fetus has full moral standing, are there situations in which its right to life is outweighed by rights of the woman, so abortion is morally permitted? If so, describe some of these situations.

Is Death Really All That Bad for You?

*I*n the movie *Annie Hall,* when Woody Allen is getting serious about Diane Keaton he wants to talk about death. So let's talk about death. But let's start with the cheery view: that it's nothing to worry about, not bad, not a harm to you at all.

This was the view of the Greek philosopher Epicurus, today remembered mainly in the names of restaurants and cookbooks. This isn't totally misguided: Epicurus thought the only good thing is pleasure, or more precisely, freedom from pain. But he wasn't a big fan of feasting and womanizing. For him the key to a happy life is philosophy, which teaches you that death isn't bad and thereby saves you needless anxieties.

To be bad for you, Epicurus argued, something has to affect your conscious experience, and in particular, cause you pain. But death can't cause you pain since when you're dead, you don't exist. (Dying can be painful, but that's different from being dead.) Death can't hurt you because you're not around to experience it. So why fret about it?

People who fear death, said Epicurus, are confused. They imagine that they'll somehow survive death, see the loss of the things they loved in life, and be pained by what they see. But this won't happen: death is only non-existence. And non-existence won't be new to us. Before we were born, we didn't exist for infinitely many years. If we don't regret this—if we don't mourn that we weren't born twenty years earlier—we shouldn't fear dying a little earlier.

When we read his arguments, we can envy Epicurus's "philosophical" attitude to his coming death. But we also think he has to be wrong. Death *is* bad, often the worst thing of all. The comforting arguments must be flawed.

Let's start by agreeing that death can only be bad for you if it affects your experiences. Granted this, death can't be bad in the way pain is, for how it feels. But it can be bad for what it prevents.

If life is good, it's so because of its pleasures and enjoyments, and death cuts these short. It prevents the good feelings you would have if you stayed alive. Death isn't bad considered by itself, but it is bad for what it disallows.

This point holds even more if, disagreeing with Epicurus, we think that things other than pleasure are good: understanding, achievement, family life. Death also stops your having more of these.

If death is just a loss, not all deaths are equally bad. Someone who dies young, with a rich life ahead of them, loses more than someone who dies at 90. And some deaths aren't bad at all. If a person's future promises only the pain of a terminal illness, dying now is merciful. But these implications seem right: our reaction to a death should depend on the alternatives to it.

The harder Epicurean argument to answer is the one about not existing before our birth. Maybe not wishing we were born earlier is irrational, and we should care more about past losses.

Maybe we find the necessary comparison impossible to make. If we'd been born twenty years earlier, we'd have been brought up in a different decade, with different interests and a different family. Who knows what our lives would have been like? Or maybe we're attached to things in this life that an earlier birth would take away, such as love for a particular person.

Epicurus's arguments can't entirely stem our fear of death: death remains a loss, sometimes an enormous one. But there's some comfort to be had. If death is just a loss, it isn't different in kind from other bad things: the rainstorm that interrupts your golf game, the bad luck that costs you a new job. It's a bigger loss, but not something unique. In Hollywood terms, death isn't like ending a movie hooked up with someone who'll make you miserable. It's more like an ending Woody Allen should be familiar with: not being hooked up with someone who would have made you happy.

QUESTIONS FOR DISCUSSION

1. How can death be bad if it's just nothingness? Isn't nothingness neither good nor bad?

2. Would you want to be immortal?

3. If not all deaths are equally bad, does it follow that not all murders are equally wrong? Is it less wrong to murder an old person with just a few years to live than to kill a healthy teenager?

Euthanasia:
Dr. Kevorkian's
Suicide Machine

*D*r. Jack Kevorkian, a retired Michigan pathologist, has invented a "suicide machine" that injects you with lethal chemicals when you press a button. On June 4, 1990, he gave this machine to Janet Adkins, a 54-year-old with Alzheimer's disease, and helped her use it to end her life. Was this an act of compassion, or was it murder?

Medical practice allows and even requires us to withhold treatment when a patient doesn't want it. If someone with a terminal illness refuses special measures to extend their life, a doctor must let them die. But Dr. Kevorkian didn't just let Mrs. Adkins die. He intervened actively to cause her death, thus participating in "active" (as opposed to "passive") euthanasia. Can this make a moral difference?

Moralities that evaluate actions only by their consequences think not. They say that if active and passive euthanasia have the same good result, namely, that someone avoids needless suffering, they are both right. And if active euthanasia produces the result more quickly, it is morally preferable.

Other moralities hold that causing evil is worse than merely allowing it to happen. If you don't save someone drowning in a river you act wrongly, but not as wrongly as if you pushed them in. For the same reason, an act with an overall good result can be wrong if it has some bad consequences and produces them in a morally forbidden way.

If the second view is correct, and causing evil is worse than allowing it, does it follow that active euthanasia is wrong? It does not, because it's not obvious that euthanasia causes any evil. This brings us to a second issue: whether our guiding value in medical ethics should be just the quality of human life — what makes life better or worse — or whether we must also value life itself, apart from its quality.

In dealing with animals, we clearly care only about their quality of life. An injured animal is put down as quickly as possible, with no thought that this may be wrong. The active killing saves the animal suffering and has no bad effects to count against this.

Those who condemn Dr. Kevorkian must have a different view about humans, treating their life as itself a value we must not destroy. They must think living itself is sacred, not just living in certain ways. But this "sanctity-of-life" view is hard to defend.

For a start, it seems to discriminate invidiously against animals. Adult humans have greater moral standing than horses, so it is usually worse to kill a human than to kill a horse. But this is because humans have qualities of mind, such as rationality and freedom, that give them a higher quality of life. To say that apart from these qualities, human life counts more seems to be rank "speciesism," the view that our species is better just because it is ours.

Religious moralists argue that human life is special because humans were created "in God's image." This argument can't be used to settle public policy in a pluralistic society, and in any case it doesn't succeed in its own terms. The Bible doesn't say that God created humans just like other animals and arbitrarily picked them as his favourite. It says he made them special by giving them distinctive qualities of mind: again, rationality and freedom. But this means that apart from those qualities, human life is not morally privileged.

Second, the sanctity-of-life view doesn't fit our reactions to deaths not involving euthanasia. Imagine that someone with a painful terminal illness dies of natural causes. If life itself were a value, our feelings should be mixed: suffering has been avoided but another great good has been lost. Yet this is not how we react. We feel simple relief, just as when an injured animal dies without needing our intervention.

Traditional Western morality says it's wrong to cause evil that good may come of it. If we accept this idea, we will think it wrong to destroy one human's quality of life to benefit others. But we need see nothing wrong in killing someone who wants to be killed and whose future offers no quality of life at all.

Dr. Kevorkian is a proselytizer for assisted suicide, and so was Mrs. Adkins: her last words were, "You must make my case known." They and their supporters can take two arguments into the public debate: that causing evil is not worse than allowing it to happen and, if that idea is too morally revolutionary, that active euthanasia properly controlled and performed in the right circumstances causes only good.

QUESTIONS FOR DISCUSSION

1. If a patient is suffering and wants to die, does it matter how their death is brought about, whether by active or passive euthanasia?

2. What does belief in the "sanctity of human life" mean, and what does it imply about the ethics of euthanasia?

3. Could there be reasons why doctor-assisted suicide, though not in itself morally wrong, should not be legally permitted?

Does Surrogate Motherhood Treat Babies and Women like Commodities?

A young woman contracts to be a surrogate mother for an infertile couple. In return for $10 000 she'll be impregnated with the husband's sperm and, after bearing a child, will surrender it to them. Is this a perversion of the birth process that should be illegal?

Much is troubling about surrogacy as practised today. It enriches lawyers, whose fees for arranging it are often higher than the birth mother's. Many women who volunteer have troubled backgrounds; motivated by feelings of inadequacy or guilt about a past abortion, they're easy prey for exploitation. After giving birth, many surrogates want to keep their babies and, when they can't, suffer considerable grief.

Regulation could minimize these problems. Surrogacies could be arranged by a non-profit state agency that screened volunteers to ensure they made rational, autonomous choices; it could also set fair fees. The surrogacy contract could even allow women to keep their babies if they wanted. (They would then forfeit their fee.)

But these changes leave untouched what, for many, is the main objection to surrogacy: that it treats children and women's labour in bearing them as commodities, as things to be bought and sold in the market. As U.S. philosopher Elizabeth Anderson says, it reduces "children to consumer durables and women to baby factories."

Statements of this objection often appeal to a moral principle proposed by the German philosopher Immanuel Kant: treat humanity "always as an end and never as a means only," or treat people always as beings owed moral respect rather than just using them for your own purposes.

Witness a British committee of inquiry that said surrogacy should be illegal because it's objectionable for some people to "treat others as means to their own ends." The committee was thinking mainly of the couple's treatment of the surrogate, but others argue that the mother treats the baby as a means—a means to making money.

These claims are too simple, though. What Kant's principle forbids isn't treating people as means but treating them *only* as means, that is, not also as ends in themselves.

In daily life we often treat people as means. At the bank we use tellers to cash cheques and make deposits. At the movies the ticket-seller is a means to admittance. None of this is wrong if we also treat these people as ends, as beings with moral standing. This happens if they benefit from interacting with us, as they do if they're paid enough and freely choose to interact.

So the question about surrogacy must be whether it treats ends *only* as means. Let's start with the couple's treatment of the surrogate. In present conditions this can violate Kant's principle. The couple, not wanting a surrogate who will change her mind, can select a woman who will be easy to manipulate and then, through their lawyer, apply pressure on her. But with proper regulation this wouldn't happen. The couple would know, from the agency, that the woman had chosen surrogacy freely, and would allow her to keep the child if surrendering it proved traumatic.

What about the mother's treatment of the child? It's morally acceptable so long as she cares in part about the child's interests; for example, about finding it a good home. This, too, the agency can handle. By screening adoptive couples, it can ensure surrogates that their children will start life well.

Some may say Kant's principle is too weak for the mother–child relationship; babies (though not adults) must be treated only as ends and never as means.

This goes too far. In the Third World, many couples have children as an economic investment; in our culture, companionship and support in old age are common motives. They're perfectly acceptable if, once the child is born, it is treated as a being owed moral respect.

There are circumstances where surrogacy could be harmful. If treating mothers and babies partly as means led us, psychologically, to view them only as means, it would be best to forbid it by law. Something like this has happened with blood donation. In Canada, blood can't be sold and the level of voluntary giving is high. The United States allows a market for blood — university students can earn money by selling plasma twice a week — and giving is much less common. That blood donation can be viewed as a means to money results in fewer choosing it for itself.

But surrogacy is unlikely to have a similar effect on childbearing. Whereas the impulse to give is fragile in humans, love of children is biologically based and strong—too strong to be displaced by a small amount of surrogacy here and there in society.

Surrogacy is different from traditional ways of giving birth, but this doesn't mean it is wrong. We have to evaluate it using our best moral principles. What these show is that surrogacy isn't wrong in principle and can be (though it isn't now) acceptable in practice.

QUESTIONS FOR DISCUSSION

1. What does it mean to treat a person "as an end" rather than "just as a means"? Is doing this an important part of treating a person morally?

2. Would allowing surrogate motherhood change the way society views women? If so, would the change be for the better or the worse?

3. If a woman wants to earn money by being a surrogate mother, does society have the right to tell her she may not do so?

If Feminists Are Pro-Choice, Why Don't They Honour Women's Choices Consistently?

*I*f Canada's feminists were really pro-choice, they wouldn't be choosy about the choices they want to protect. They'd trust and respect women always, not just when they're making choices about abortions.

Most feminists assume that a fetus has no moral standing, so the only person directly affected by a decision about abortion is the woman. And they think the woman should be allowed to make this decision herself. She should be legally entitled to an abortion whatever her reason for wanting it.

One possible justification for this stand is that a woman is the best judge of her interests. She knows more about herself and her situation than any doctor or bureaucrat, and can make a wiser decision. A different justification is that, even if she isn't the best judge, it's her life and she's entitled to make choices about it.

But these justifications are hard to reconcile with other feminist stands. In a brief to the Royal Commission on New Reproductive Technologies, the National Action Committee on the Status of Women called for a moratorium on opening new in vitro fertilization clinics. It argues that in vitro fertilization is bad for women: it has a low success rate and can have dangerous side effects. But if women are wise enough or entitled to judge their own interests in abortion cases, why not also here?

Using in vitro fertilization can have far-reaching consequences, but so can a choice about abortion. A woman who has an abortion can feel remorse in later years. A young woman who does not have an abortion can drop out of high school, go on welfare, and limit her opportunities for the rest of her life. Yet NAC opposes even the mild interference with these women's freedom of requiring them to get counselling before they make their choices. (The call for counselling usually comes from pro-life groups, but there could just as well be feminist counselling.)

The brief to the royal commission also opposes surrogate motherhood, which NAC wants to see banned. But what if a woman freely chooses to be a surrogate, in return for a reasonable fee? If all abortion decisions are voluntary, surely this decision can sometimes be voluntary. Feminists would presumably likewise oppose any proposal to legalize polygamy. But if a woman chooses to enter a polygamous marriage, shouldn't her choice deserve respect?

Some feminists recognize these tensions and try to separate a woman's choice about abortion from these other choices. The first, they say, is genuinely private, affecting only the woman herself; the others have a larger public aspect.

This is hard to argue for in the case of in vitro fertilization, but it may be plausible for surrogate motherhood and polygamy. To legalize these practices, it may be said, is to reinforce social perceptions of women as inferior and as tied to breeding, and to compound the harms these perceptions do. But this is a dangerous argument.

To believe in choice is to believe that people should be allowed to make decisions about their own lives, and this requires drawing a strict boundary around their lives. It disallows such arguments as: abortion isn't a private choice because a woman having an abortion sets a bad example for other women. Nor does it allow arguments about remote or indirect effects on society. Allow these, and nothing counts as a private choice.

As always, we have to ask of a feminist argument: would its proponents accept a similar argument about abortion?

Let's go back to the young woman who drops out of high school to have a baby. She, too, sets a bad example for others — the more women choose to limit their opportunities, the more normal their choice looks and the more women will follow their path. And she contributes to a social perception of women as tied to breeding. If effects like these are reasons for banning surrogacy and polygamy, why not also for interfering with her choice to have her baby? Or if her choice must be utterly unrestricted, why not other choices too?

Canada's feminists face their own choice: either they trust and respect women, in which case they should honour women's choices consistently; or they think women need protection and coddling at the hands of Big Sister.

QUESTIONS FOR DISCUSSION

1. Why, if at all, should society leave people free to make choices about their own lives?

2. Is it true that people's choices should never be restricted because of "remote or indirect" effects on society? Discuss with reference not just to abortion and surrogate motherhood, but also to issues such as gun control and the restriction of pornography.

3. Could a feminist argue that abortion and new reproductive technologies are sufficiently different issues that a pro-choice position is appropriate on the one but not the other?

Tailoring Our Genes: The Ethics of Genetic Engineering

*T*he cloning of Dolly the sheep in 1997 was followed the next year by the cloning of over 50 mice. In the meantime the Human Genome Project, seeking to identify all the genes in human DNA, moves steadily forward. The time may not be far off when human genetic engineering is a real possibility. Would it be right, or horribly wrong, to use our knowledge to change people's genes?

The less controversial possibility is negative genetic engineering: repairing a defective gene to stop a specific disease. It can take two forms. In "somatic" gene therapy, you change just part of the body. If a disease is localized in the bone marrow, for example, you alter the cells there but not elsewhere, and the change isn't passed on to the patient's offspring. More radical is "germline" therapy: changing the DNA in sperm or egg cells before they fertilize. If a flawed gene is fixed here, the change is transmitted to future generations.

Both procedures have obvious risks: who knows what other effects changing a gene will have? But these are reasons for caution, not an outright ban. If we knew that somatic therapy to cure cystic fibrosis had no side effects, who could be against it? We're pleased to have eliminated smallpox for future generations; why not also eliminate a genetic disease?

What is more controversial is positive genetic engineering: using gene therapy not just to overcome defects but to improve the species, by making us taller, smarter, kinder. It conjures up visions of the Nazi eugenics program or Aldous Huxley's *Brave New World*, where workers are bred to be happy with menial work.

With positive genetic engineering, the risks are even greater. The gene for cystic fibrosis is comparatively simple; that for selfishness is surely complex. And there are worries about the wrong "improvements" being made: parents wanting only boys, or scientists boosting intelligence so much that all human feeling gets lost.

English philosopher Jonathan Glover, a cautious proponent of positive engineering, proposes a "mixed" system to minimize these worries. In this system, the initiative for genetic change rests with parents but must then be approved by a central authority. There are two checks on bad genetic change: the concern of parents for their children and that of the state for the social good. The first protects against a race of menial workers, the second against a generation programmed just to make money.

For many, the objections to positive genetic engineering go deeper. Isn't it presumptuous, they ask, to think we know what an "improvement" is, or what would make the species "better"?

But we do know this when we bring up our children. We give them an education so they'll understand themselves and the world; we try to make them caring and responsible. If we can use values in changing our children's environment, why not also when changing their genes?

Sometimes the objection is that positive engineering involves "playing God," or meddling where we shouldn't. This too is a bad argument.

For one thing, we "play God" every time we avoid a falling rock or take medicine: we change the course of nature because we don't like where it's going. And in rejecting positive engineering we'd still be making a choice. We'd be preferring the genetic status quo to any alternative, and why think the status quo is best? We have the traits we have because they've proved useful to a bunch of selfish genes. Why think the results of that process are morally ideal?

A look around us is hardly encouraging. As Jonathan Glover says, a ban on positive engineering "will seem an acceptable option to all those who can watch the news on television and feel satisfied with the world. It will appeal to those who can talk to their children about the history of the twentieth century without wishing they could leave some things out."

Genetic engineering is like nuclear technology: it can be used for evil, but it can also be used for good—perhaps tremendous good. We must absolutely be cautious in trying new techniques, but those techniques may one day offer a glorious opportunity. It would be wonderful if, through moral and social reform, human beings became kinder, more sensitive, and less grasping. It would also be good if we got that way by changing our genes.

QUESTIONS FOR DISCUSSION

1. Does genetic engineering differ fundamentally or in kind from traditional medical practices, or does it differ only in degree?

2. What assumptions are implicit in the argument that genetic engineering involves "playing God"? Are these assumptions reasonable?

3. Do parents have the right to determine (within limits) what genes their children will have, or does that violate their children's right to autonomy?

Part Three

Environmental Ethics

*T*here are many pressing problems about the environment: air and water pollution, ozone depletion, global warming. But to know what response to these problems is ethically right, we have to resolve a more abstract issue: do our duties concerning the environment derive only from the interests of humans, either present or future, or do we have duties to care about aspects of the environment — animals, plants, ecosystems — for their own sakes? The essays to follow examine this question and its implications for debates about vegetarianism, global warming, and planetary engineering.

Why Many Find Meat-Eating Hard to Digest

*D*ining with philosophers has always been difficult. First there's picking a restaurant, a subject on which they have absurdly strong views. Then there are the ethicists with their complicated theories of fairness. ("I didn't like my shrimp, so I should pay less than the menu price, but you said your salmon was very good.") In the past decade there's been a more serious concern: accommodating the many philosophers who are now vegetarians.

Among Canadian philosophers, perhaps 10 to 15 percent eat no meat. This isn't a fad or the sign of midlife worries about health. They've been convinced by moral arguments that it's wrong to eat animals. And those who haven't changed eating habits — like me — have the shaming thought that what we're doing is indefensible.

One argument for vegetarianism is its effect on other humans. It can take up to 21 pounds of grain protein fed to a feedlot calf to produce a single pound of meat protein for humans. In a world where millions are starving, this is a colossally inefficient approach to agriculture. If North Americans reduced their meat consumption by 10 percent for one year, this would free enough grain to feed 65 million people.

A second argument concerns the suffering inflicted on animals by modern factory farming. A veal calf spends its entire life in a stall less than 60 cm wide, unable to move or even adopt its natural sleeping position. To keep its meat light-coloured — something unrelated to its taste — the calf is denied nutrients such as iron. Craving these nutrients, it licks any metal fittings on its stall.

In the most intensive operations, broiler chickens are confined in cages whose wire floors cut their feet. They spend their entire lives in a space no bigger than a single piece of typing paper. Stressed by overcrowding, the birds peck at and even kill each other. (The farmer's solution to this problem: cut off their beaks when they're young.)

Sometimes suffering is justified by later benefits, but here the benefits are morally trivial. Unlike wolves or lions, we humans don't need meat for a healthy diet. And the pleasures of the table surely don't justify torturing animals throughout their lives.

The idea needn't be that animals are the same as humans or have exactly the same rights. We humans can have more complex pleasures and pains; we're also capable of rationality and free choice. But whenever a human, whatever its other capacities, suffers pain, that's morally bad. It should be the same in other species.

The argument also allows a principled distinction between what may and may not be eaten, based on the capacity for suffering. There's nothing wrong with eating plants, since they have no sensations. And if oysters, clams, and mussels don't feel pain, eating them is fine too. Shrimp, crabs, and lobster apparently suffer, as do fish, birds, and mammals.

A more simple-looking argument for vegetarianism — that meat-eating involves killing animals — is more controversial.

Imagine that farming was more humane, that animals roamed free, enjoying several months or years of pleasant life before being painlessly killed. Here killing would deprive them of more pleasant years. But this wouldn't be wrong, one might argue, because the prospect of being killed was necessary for them to be bred and thus to exist at all. Our meat-eating would give them some pleasant years, which is at least no worse than none.

As critics point out, we'd never accept this argument about humans. If we developed a taste for babies' flesh, we couldn't justify breeding and killing them on the ground that otherwise they wouldn't be born. But maybe animals, though they have some moral standing, don't have all the standing of humans. Maybe what's wrong to do to humans isn't wrong to do to beings that can never have free choice.

This issue, however intricate philosophically, is for practical purposes moot. Current farming techniques do cause suffering to animals, either when they're being raised or when they're transported and slaughtered. In these conditions, many philosophers have decided that eating meat is wrong. This has meant a small increase in business for Thai, Indian, and Greek restaurants, and a small dent in the earnings of steakhouses.

QUESTIONS FOR DISCUSSION

1. Do we have duties to animals, or should we view them just as existing to satisfy our needs?

2. Can one defend meat-eating by arguing that if wolves and lions aren't morally wrong to eat meat, neither can humans be wrong?

3. Would meat-eating be morally acceptable if animals were treated humanely while alive and then killed painlessly, or would the killing still be wrong?

Should the West Pay for China's Fridges?

*R*ight now, China's 1.2 billion people don't own refrigerators. But what if they get them, as China's government plans, and the country's per capita fridge ownership comes to equal that in the West? Who will pay for China's refrigerators?

If the refrigerators are of the traditional freon-cooled type, the whole world will pay. Freon is a chlorofluorocarbon, and CFCs damage the earth's ozone layer. They're also responsible for about 15 percent of the global warming trend known as the greenhouse effect. If China gets freon-cooled refrigerators, we'll all pay in increased cancers, dried out farming regions, and rising ocean levels.

Alerted to the dangers of CFCs, Western governments have proposed international action to eliminate them. Forty countries agreed in Montreal in 1987 to halve CFC production by 1998; now they've agreed to a complete ban. The West wants all countries to eliminate CFCs before the century ends.

To the West's surprise, Third World countries, including China, have rejected these proposals as unfair. The developed world, they say, was able to industrialize using cheap materials such as CFCs. Now that the Third World stands poised for its own industrialization, it's not fair to ask it to use what are bound to be more expensive substitutes. It's not fair to delay even further its economic betterment.

Third World countries don't refuse to use substitutes for CFCs; they just want the developed world to pay them the difference between the cost of these substitutes and the CFCs they give up.

Should the West pay for China's refrigerators? There are many moral arguments why we should. Helping China would be kind, an act of generosity; it would also reduce international inequality. But these are not ideas to which our governments have traditionally given much credence, as their tiny foreign aid budgets attest. Are there reasons for paying that are more attuned to our governments' moral thinking?

Some say there are. Third World countries, they argue, wouldn't be in the position they're in now if the developed countries hadn't already damaged the ozone layer with their own CFCs. So, the developed countries owe the Third World compensation. They're responsible for the Third World's having to use more expensive materials and must therefore pay the extra cost of these materials.

This argument seems to have won a convert in former British prime minister Margaret Thatcher. At a conference about the ozone problem, she said it would be "intolerable" if the countries "which have already industrialized, and which have caused the greater part of the problems we face" expected others to pay to solve them.

Perhaps Mrs. Thatcher shouldn't have been so easily convinced. The harm to Third World countries wasn't done in the way normally required for compensation. Compensation is normally owed only for acts of negligence or carelessness. If, because of my careless driving, my car leaves the road and hits you on the sidewalk, I owe you compensation for your injuries. But if I drive as safely as possible and hit an unforeseeable patch of ice with the same result, I don't owe compensation. The patch of ice was bad luck; the bad luck ended up harming you; but since I wasn't at fault in what happened, I'm not liable for damages.

The developed world, it can be argued, is in the position of a driver who's skidded on unforeseeable ice.

When Kelvinator marketed the first refrigerator in 1918, it had no idea its product could damage the ozone layer. When Styrofoam was introduced, there was no evidence it would increase global temperatures. Although actions in the West have harmed the Third World, no one was at fault in most of those actions, and therefore no compensation is owed. The Third World's position is largely bad luck — unfortunate, but not something that calls for special aid.

Where does this leave us? Without the argument about compensation we face a moral choice. If our governments retain their old moral ideas, we'll ask China to buy costlier refrigerators and fall farther behind in economic development, all to protect our common environment. We may be unable to bring ourselves to this. But if we can't, as Mrs. Thatcher apparently couldn't, we'll have to change our moral thinking. We'll have to start caring more about international giving or equality for their own sake. And this will have far-reaching consequences.

Arguments about equality, for example, don't apply just to CFC substitutes; they support a general program of international redistribution. To accept them in one area is implicitly to accept a shift in all our dealings with poorer countries.

The issue of China's refrigerators foreshadows many the world will face in coming decades. We need to switch from damaging technologies to ones that are environmentally safer but also, inevitably, more expensive. This will repeatedly raise the question of who will pay the extra cost of these technologies in developing countries. And this question poses a moral challenge. Will we retain our old moral ideas, and ask the least well off countries to pay the most for environmental protection? Or will we find in the environment the beginnings of a new concern for global equality?

QUESTIONS FOR DISCUSSION

1. Is it fair to ask Third World countries to slow down their economic development to protect an environment already ravaged by developed countries?

2. Since Western countries now know about the bad effects of CFCs, will they owe compensation for harms arising from their use of CFCs from now into the future?

3. What is the ethically ideal level of human damage to the environment? Is zero damage ideal, or would it be wrong to reduce polluting activities as much as that target requires?

If Human Life Is a Good Thing, Why Worry about the Population Explosion?

*T*he planet is getting crowded. The United Nations recently warned that the world's population is growing faster than predicted. It will probably pass 5.4 billion this summer and could be 10 billion by 2050.

Our first reaction is to see this simply as bad. Famines often happen because there are more mouths than the local economy can feed. And more people means more stress on the environment: more cars driven, more electricity generated, more forests cut down — all reasons to want the growth stopped.

But wait. If human life is a good thing — and it must be, if killing is wrong — shouldn't more of it be even better? Shouldn't we want more people to enjoy life? The idea wouldn't be to increase the population no matter what; we also care about the quality of human life. But we could treat a larger population as one good thing to be weighed against others.

Yet we don't do this. Many people think a reasonable population policy is zero population growth. And a U.S. Senate commission has said "there would be no substantial benefits from the continued growth of the U.S. population." It counted as nothing the benefits to the extra Americans who would get some life rather than none.

We could try to justify this thinking by saying there's never a moral reason to create human beings. We ought to ensure a decent quality of life for people who will live no matter what we do, but we have no duty to bring people into existence. As Canadian philosopher Jan Narveson puts it, morality tells us to make people happy, not to make happy people.

This theory fits our everyday thinking about having babies. If a couple who could conceive a happy child choose not to, we don't think they've acted wrongly.

But the theory also faces problems. Imagine that a couple knowingly conceive a child who will be miserable, so much so that it would be better off not living. Surely this is wrong. But how can a child's future pain be a reason against conceiving it when its future happiness isn't a reason in favour of conceiving it?

The theory also has an implication that many (though not Professor Narveson) would find unacceptable: that there's nothing wrong in letting the human race die out. Imagine that everyone joins in a pact to stop procreating; maybe there's a drug that makes you infertile, and everyone takes the drug. If there is no duty to conceive children, there's nothing wrong with this pact. Yet many of us find it appalling.

We need a compromise theory. Because human life is a good thing, it's morally important that there be some of it. That's why letting the race die out would be dreadful. And when the population is small, increasing it is a priority, even at some cost to people's quality of life.

(In a teenage boy's fantasy, you're the sole male survivor of a nuclear holocaust, surrounded by beautiful women and with the delicious duty to procreate. I'm suggesting this fantasy has a sound ethical basis.)

But as the population grows, the moral importance of adding to it gets smaller and eventually becomes negligible. There is "diminishing marginal value" in extra people. When the population is as large as it is now, over five billion, additions count almost nothing against effects on the average quality of life. Assuming there will be a reasonable number of people in the future, increases that lower the average happiness are wrong.

This theory brings our thinking about our own population into line with our thinking about other species. We think it's important that there be some whooping cranes in the world, and when the number gets low we spend considerable sums to increase it. But if the number reached several million, we would stop. Having some cranes is important, but more than enough is enough. And we should take the same view about humans.

So we should worry about rapid population growth and do what we can to stop it. The reason isn't that it's never good to create more human beings; it's that it isn't good now. When God told Adam and Eve to "go forth and multiply," there were only two of them. He wouldn't give the same command today.

QUESTIONS FOR DISCUSSION

1. How might one argue that zero population growth is the ideal population policy?

2. If everyone voluntarily agreed to let the human race die out, would that be morally wrong?

3. Some countries, for instance, China, legally forbid couples to have more than a specified number of children, such as one or two. Is this a laudable effort at population control or a violation of parents' rights to make free choices about procreation?

Should We Implant Life on Mars?

*T*here were no little green men. In fact, when the Mars Pathfinder mission visited Mars in 1997, there were no signs of any life at all, just a cold, barren planet. But whether there *is* life on Mars isn't the only interesting question. Another is whether there *should be*. If we could put life on Mars, by implanting it or helping it develop, would that be ethically right?

The science of this issue has been explored by NASA scientists in the United States. Though Mars is cold now, it was warmer in the past and could be made warmer again. The earth's atmosphere is warm partly because of greenhouse gases such as carbon dioxide; we could inject some of those gases into Mars's atmosphere to get the same effect. In addition, huge mirrors could be placed in orbit around Mars's poles. At the right angles they could melt the planet's ice caps and stop them from reflecting heat back into space. If Mars were warmed in these ways, two things might follow.

It may be that when Mars was warmer, life was already developing. (Some scientists believe a

Martian asteroid found in Antarctica contains evidence of just such long-ago life.) If so, the warming might unfreeze this life. If not, we could take life to Mars. We could implant micro-organisms selected or genetically engineered to fit the new Martian environment and let them develop. Either way, a process of evolution could begin that would eventually give Mars a rich and varied set of life forms.

Since this project would be fantastically expensive, it might be wrong so long as there were more pressing human needs on Earth. But let's set that aside and consider the project just in itself. Costs aside, would implanting life on Mars be ethically right? This question pulls apart two ideas commonly run together in contemporary thinking about the environment.

One idea is that humans should respect nature as it is, not interfering with natural processes or trying to impose our values on them. The other is that we should appreciate nature for its vitality, richness, and delicate balancing of life forms.

These ideas lead to the same conclusions about many contemporary environmental issues such as preserving the tropical rain forest. There, nature as it is is vital and diverse; nature as it would be after human intervention is barren and shorn of unique species.

But the ideas come apart when we think about implanting life on Mars. The first idea says this would be wrong, a violation of Mars's integrity as a dead planet. Any life resulting from such elaborate technology would be unnatural and therefore bad. The second idea says that if diversity is good on Earth, it is good everywhere; we should enliven Mars, not for our sake, but to give it an intrinsically better environment.

Thinking about Mars can therefore help us decide which of the two environmental ideas is more important. I think it's clear it's the second idea, about the value of diversity everywhere.

That's something's unnatural in the sense of artificial can't mean that it's in itself bad. Are medicines bad if they're invented by humans? Must we refuse to cure a disease if the cure relies on science? Nor is there any reason to believe that natural processes always produce what by independent criteria is best. This must often happen; the flourishing of life shows that. But the same nature that creates life creates storms and earthquakes that destroy it. If Harvard paleontologist Stephen Jay Gould is right, the trend of evolution has been to reduce genetic diversity; there are fewer kinds of life than 550 million years ago. In the very long run, nature will heat the Sun and destroy all life on Earth.

So sometimes nature produces what's bad and technology can produce something better. And isn't a vital and varied Mars better than one that's barren? Surely a universe with life on two planets is better than a universe with life on only one. This is especially so if the two kinds of life are different, because evolution on the two planets has taken a different course. This opens up an exciting prospect for the future of humankind. If we solve our problems on Earth, however many centuries that takes, we can turn our attention to the universe, taking the life that makes our environment so valuable to other planets and galaxies.

In thinking ethically about the environment, we have to use our own values, that is, our own ideas about what's good. These values need not be human-centred. They can agree that animals' lives are morally important just as humans' are. They can also agree with "deep ecology" that there's intrinsic worth in ecosystems and other larger features of the non-human environment. But they have to be our values, and they can sometimes justify interfering with natural processes.

This can be hard to see in our current situation, where the most common effect of technology is to destroy the environment. But technology can also be used to preserve environmental value from forces that would destroy it. (If we could somehow stop the heating of the Sun, would that not be right?) It can even be used, with the appropriate caution of course, to create such value. This is clearest on other planets such as Mars. Though now of little or no environmental worth, they could have considerable value. If we put that value there, that would be a wonderful achievement.

QUESTIONS FOR DISCUSSION

1. Does Mars have any value in its present state, or without life is it completely valueless?

2. Would it be better if life developed naturally on Mars than after human intervention? If humans did intervene, would it be better if they merely unfroze existing Martian life and let it continue its development than if they took the first life to Mars?

3. Are there any cases on Earth where technology could increase environmental value, that is, increase the vitality and diversity of life-forms? If so, would it be right to use the technology for this purpose?

Part Four

The Nature of Morality

This part doesn't so much engage in moral reasoning as ask some abstract questions about it: What is the relationship between morality and religion? Are values relative? Should the moral life be easy or hard? These are classical philosophical questions about the nature of morality — not about what's right and wrong, but about what we are doing and how we should proceed when we think about what's right and wrong.

Values Are Not Relative

𝒫eople disagree about moral issues. In our own culture, some people think abortion is a woman's right while others think it's murder. Some think homosexuality is a terrible sin; others think it's fine. There can be even bigger disagreements between cultures, say, between Canada and Iran, or Canada and a jungle tribe in Africa.

Some people think this disagreement shows there can't be an objective, universal morality. If there were such a morality, wouldn't we all agree about what it says? If we don't agree, doesn't that show that the idea of such a morality is an illusion? These people are led to the position of *moral relativism*: what's right and wrong isn't objective but varies from person to person. If you think homosexuality is wrong, then it's wrong for you, but if you think it's fine, it's fine for you. Equality for women may be right in Canada but wrong in Iran or in the jungle tribe.

This moral relativism sounds modern and progressive, but it's not coherent and it's not what anyone really believes. Nor can it even make sense of the moral disagreement it sets out to explain.

Let's start with what follows from relativism. Some people say that if morality is relative, then we shouldn't impose our own values on other people. We shouldn't impose our beliefs about which sexual practices are wrong, because for others those practices may be right. And we should be tolerant of other cultures, letting them live by their own values rather than forcing them to adopt ours.

This ideal of tolerance is, at least to a point, attractive. But it actually contradicts relativism. That's because the ideal is presented as one that's binding on everyone: everyone in every culture should refrain from imposing their values. But that's a universal and objective statement! What a consistent relativism implies is that if you think being tolerant is right then it's right for you, but if you think forcing other people to live by your values is right then that's right too. If relativists don't say this — if they call for tolerance from everyone — they don't really believe what relativism says.

In fact, none of us believe what relativism says. A consistent relativism implies that if you think murder is wrong, then it's wrong for you, but if you think it's right, it's right. Likewise for rape, torture, or anything else. In fact, relativism says that if you think torturing millions of people to death for your own amusement is right, then it's right for you and no one can criticize your action. Does anyone remotely believe that?

The popularity of relativism stems partly from a mistaken interpretation of a recent change in moral beliefs. Many traditional moralities contain rules governing your private life, where what you do affects only yourself or others with their agreement. For example, they contain rules forbidding sexual practices such as homosexuality, even among consenting adults. A newer "permissive" morality says there are no rules about your private life. If what you do doesn't harm others, then it can't be right or wrong. In that sphere, everything is morally permitted.

This permissive morality looks relativistic but isn't, in two ways. First, its permissive claims concern only your private life and not actions that affect others. Those actions, such as murder and rape, can still be wrong for everyone everywhere. Second, even its permissive claims are universal. They say that homosexuality among consenting adults is neither right nor wrong but permitted for everyone. If someone thinks her engaging in homosexuality would be wrong, then she doesn't believe something that's true for her. She believes something that's false.

Moral relativism, then, has implications none of us believe. And it also can't explain why we take morality as seriously as we do.

Return to a moral disagreement, say, about abortion. If relativism were true, then a pro-lifer's claim that abortion is wrong would mean only that the pro-lifer's having an abortion would be wrong for her. And a pro-choicer's claim that abortion is a woman's right would mean only that the pro-choicer's having an abortion would not be wrong for her. But those two claims aren't in disagreement! Since each claim talks about a different person's actions, they don't conflict. For there to be conflict, or any point to a disagreement about abortion, each side's claims must concern the moral status of abortion for all people everywhere. But that is what relativism says they cannot do.

Or consider our own moral deliberations. We often think it's important to have the soundest moral opinions, and spend time and energy trying to identify what they are. But if relativism were true, this would be pointless. Let's say that at one time I believe abortion is wrong. Then according to relativism, abortion is wrong for me then and my not having an abortion is right. But later I change my mind and come to believe that abortion is right; now my having an abortion is right for me. Whatever my moral beliefs, my acting on those beliefs is right. So why care about what moral beliefs I have? Just as we can only explain moral disagreements by assuming that moral beliefs make universal claims, so we can only see a point in moral thinking given the same non-relativistic assumption.

What, then, about the moral disagreement that leads so many people to embrace relativism? Isn't it inconsistent with an objective, universal morality? I think we have to see moral issues as hard, ones it takes lots of thought to get right. It took humankind centuries to discover that slavery is wrong. A practice that now strikes us as obviously heinous was accepted by morally sensitive people in ancient Greece and by millions of North Americans just 150 years ago. But if it was hard to work out the morality of slavery, how much harder can it be to decide about abortion or genetic engineering? So even if we make progress, there may be disagreements, and heated ones, along the way. But they'll be, as they have to be, disagreements about what is right for all people everywhere.

QUESTIONS FOR DISCUSSION

1. To what extent should we be tolerant of other cultures, letting them live by their own values rather than judging them by ours? Is this tolerance always demanded, or can it be taken too far?

2. Is it true that morality makes different claims about our private lives than about actions that affect other people? Or is there no sphere where everything is morally permitted?

3. If we disagree about what is objectively right on issues such as abortion, is there a way we could work toward agreement? Is there a strategy for reaching consensus on hard moral questions?

Should Morality Be a Struggle? Ancient vs. Modern Ideas about Ethics

*I*magine that two accountants do similar jobs for similar companies. One day they make the same discovery: with almost no chance of getting caught, they can embezzle a large sum from their employers. They can both use the money, to pay off debts or buy a new car.

The first accountant right away says to himself, "It's wrong to steal," and never considers the matter again. But the second accountant is torn. She, too, knows stealing is wrong, but she's tempted and at first decides to go ahead. Then she decides she won't, and then that she will. Finally, after weeks of agonizing, she decides not to embezzle. Who is the morally better person?

My fellow students and I were asked this at the start of an undergraduate seminar on Aristotle. The point wasn't that there was a single right answer we had to give; it was to highlight differences between ancient and modern views of ethics.

Aristotle and most other Greek philosophers would have said the first accountant is better, because he has a harmonious personality. He has correct beliefs about what's right and no appetites or impulses that conflict with them. He's integrated, stable, at one with his moral convictions.

Aristotle thought this kind of harmony was essential to true virtue. The virtuous person would, for example, be moderate about sensual pleasures, but he wouldn't find this difficult. He would dislike the taste of rich or unhealthy foods; he'd get no enjoyment from adultery even if he happened to try it.

The Greeks could value inner harmony because they assumed that morality and self-interest go hand in hand. The second accountant is tempted to embezzle the money because she thinks this will benefit her. But Aristotle would say this is a mistake. What's really in your interest is leading the best life, which is a life of virtue and excludes stealing. To be tempted is to be confused.

Modern ethics is more sympathetic to the second accountant. We doubt whether virtue in Aristotle's sense is attainable; we think of morality as a struggle against evil or selfish impulses that we can't get rid of but can only restrain. (Think of dieting as portrayed in the "Cathy" comic strip. It's a battle against cravings for chocolate, ice cream, and the like. Wrongdoing strikes us as similarly delicious.)

This modern picture has partly religious origins. The Christian doctrine of original sin says that, after the fall in the Garden of Eden, all humans are corrupted. We have within us tendencies to evil that cannot be eliminated ("the old Adam") and against which we must constantly struggle. As St. Paul said, "The flesh lusteth against the spirit," and the best we can do is lust back against it.

But there are secular versions of the same idea. Our twentieth-century psychologies teach us that we have inborn tendencies, the products now of biology rather than divinity, to pleasure, aggression, or dominance. They're the nasty, uncivilized part of our nature, and though they can be diverted, sublimated, or restrained, they can't be eliminated. The moral life, again, is a struggle against oneself.

Like the Greek picture, this modern one is tied to beliefs about morality and self-interest. But where the Greeks assume that doing what's right is the same as benefiting yourself, we think the two clash. Morality involves a sacrifice of your interests for other people's, and that's what makes it hard.

This makes us suspicious of the first accountant. Doesn't his easy virtue look like a mindless following of rules whose costs he doesn't really understand? Morality does require giving up your interests, and the second accountant's struggle reflects this. But the first accountant seems to ignore this, or to be missing some basic drives.

Our modern picture of morality is grim, in contrast with the light, harmonious picture Aristotle paints. But sometimes reality is more hard than beautiful. The German philosopher G.W.F. Hegel said that Greek civilization expressed a beautiful naïvete, treating in simple harmony what we see as opposed. You can see this in Greek ethics. There virtue is effortless because it's good for you—but we find it a struggle.

QUESTIONS FOR DISCUSSION

1. Who is more admirable, the first accountant or the second?

2. Is virtue in Aristotle's sense of inner harmony
    attainable, or do we all have nasty tendencies
    that can never be eliminated but at best con-
    trolled?

3. Is Aristotle right that a life can't be the best if
    it involves acting unethically, or does ethical
    action sometimes require sacrificing even your
    ultimate interests?

Why God Is Irrelevant to Morality

"**If** God is dead, everything is permitted." That's what Ivan says in Dostoevsky's *The Brothers Karamazov* and what many people believe: without religion there's no basis for morality. I believe the opposite: that moral issues can be discussed in a purely secular way. It's an age-old issue in philosophy.

At first sight, morality and religion seem easy to separate. Many atheists have moral principles and act on them conscientiously. Some even accept the principles of religious morality non-religiously. They believe that Jesus, for example, was a great moral teacher but insist he was a human teacher, not divine.

Those who tie ethics to religion don't deny these obvious facts. They claim instead that morality without religion, though possible, is irrational — something you might go for if naïve or deluded but not if you saw clearly what the "death of God" implies.

One argument for this is that we need God to reward virtue and punish vice in the afterlife.

Otherwise, being moral is not in our long-term self-interest and is therefore irrational.

This argument assumes that we're always motivated by self-interest — which we're not. We can care directly about other people just as, when angry, we can want to hurt them regardless of the effect on us. We can also be moved just by the thought that something is right. If we are, and we act on this motive, we're perfectly rational.

In any case, pursuing self-interest in the suggested way won't work. In most religions, whether you're saved depends on your motives: you have to act from love or from a desire to do your duty. If your goal is only heaven for yourself, you won't get there.

The more serious argument tying ethics to religion concerns not the motive for morality, but its possibility. If God exists, it's said, then moral principles have reality as his commands or the decrees of his will. If he doesn't, they're phantoms, will-o'-the-wisps, nothing. This is the core idea of religious ethics: something's being right just is its being commanded by God. So without God, rightness is impossible.

This idea was refuted 2500 years ago by Socrates. In a dialogue of Plato's called the *Euthyphro*, he shows decisively why religion is not only unnecessary for but irrelevant to morality.

Imagine that God gives us certain commands, for example, to love our neighbours as ourselves. Why, Socrates asks, does God give these commands and not others? Is it because they're morally right, or for some other reason? Either answer lands religious ethics in a pickle.

If God commands acts because they're right, then the acts are right apart from his will, and morality is real independently of God. But if he doesn't command acts because they're right, we have no moral reason to obey him. God has impressive qualities: he's all-powerful, all-knowing, creator of the universe. But these qualities are compatible with moral evil. Unless we know independently that his commands are right, obeying him is just blind submission to authority.

We can rationally follow God's commands, Socrates shows, but only after using our own moral judgment. Our reasoning can't be, "He's God, therefore what he says is right." It must be, "What he says is right, therefore he is or may be God."

A defender of religious ethics may object that this ignores a crucial fact: God's infinite goodness. The gods Socrates knew, the petty, squabbling gods of Olympus, weren't good and there was no reason to obey them. But the Christian god is perfectly virtuous.

This addition doesn't change the argument. We have to ask whether God's goodness constrains him, so there are things he couldn't command and still be good, or does not. If it does constrain him, God couldn't command hating one's neighbour and still be good. But this means that hating one's neighbour is wrong in itself, that is, that morality exists apart from God. If God's goodness does not constrain him, he could command anything — but then we have no moral reason to obey him. Doing so is again just blind loyalty, closer to Nuremberg than to Nazareth.

Socrates's argument doesn't deny that religion can be important psychologically, in forming an attachment to morality. Many children first come to respect morality by associating it with an all-powerful authority figure. An adult's moral resolve can be strengthened by thoughts of a divine commander and his rewards and punishments.

But let's be clear. If we rely on these religious props — and pessimists say we need them to avoid sliding into moral laxness — it's only because we're irrational. It's because we can't act morally for the one good reason for doing so, namely, that

it's right to so act regardless of anyone's com-
mandments. If God exists, he can't make things
right that aren't already so. If he doesn't exist, this
doesn't morally make a difference.

QUESTIONS FOR DISCUSSION

1. If there was a god who rewarded virtue and
    punished vice in an afterlife, would this
    change the reasons you have for acting
    morally, say, for helping a person in need?

2. Socrates argues that we can only know
    whether God's commands are worth obeying if
    we know, independently, that what God com-
    mands is right. Does this argument claim,
    arrogantly, to know more than God does?

3. If religion is irrelevant to morality, why has
    religion been so important in the development
    of morality?

The Problem of Evil: Looking Rationally at the World, You Can't Be a Christian

*F*or Voltaire, it was an earthquake at Lisbon in 1755; for Bertrand Russell it was fascism and the Ku Klux Klan. Both men saw evil in the world, and couldn't believe in a Christian god.

According to Christian teaching, the world was created by a god who is all-powerful and perfectly good. This creates a certain expectation: that the world will be a decent place. That it seems wretched, instead, is the theological "problem of evil."

This problem wasn't invented by unbelievers such as Voltaire. It has long been known to Christian apologists, who try to solve it by showing that evil can be a means to a greater good. They have two cases to consider: *moral evil*, or nastiness in our choices and character, and the *physical evil* of pain, suffering, and disease.

Moral evil looks like the easier of the two. In creating us "in his image," apologists say, God made humans free, and with freedom comes the possibility of sin. Freedom is a great good, and the precondition for moral virtue. But God couldn't give it to us without allowing us to choose vice.

It's not clear, though, that this argument lets God off the hook. Couldn't he create beings who were free but always acted virtuously? Christians believe that God himself is like this: free but always willing what's right. And many believe that in heaven the saved will always freely choose what's right. So why couldn't God make us that way from the start?

Whatever we think about moral evil, the tougher case is physical evil. That's what got to Voltaire about the Lisbon earthquake: needless suffering in no way caused by human wrongdoing. But again, there are arguments why the evil serves a greater good.

It's said, for example, that we learn from pain, our disappointments leading us to greater strengths. More generally, pain is a warning system, telling us when our bodies are threatened. In implanting this system in us, God was caring for our greater welfare.

This argument insults God, for it ignores his omnipotence. Maybe we humans, limited by the laws of the world and our psychology, can't be warned of dangers except by pain. But God is above those laws. He created them; and why couldn't he create different laws? Why couldn't he create beings who were sufficiently alerted to injuries by digital readouts or flashing lights, and never had to suffer pain?

A more serious argument is that physical evil is necessary for there to be moral good. Without pain there could be no courage, compassion, and heroic struggle, and these virtues are the crown of creation. Yes, there's evil in the world, but it allows the greater good of moral triumph over it.

Again the argument is flawed. For one, it isn't relevant to the huge quantity of suffering that doesn't give rise to any virtue. Imagine someone crushed under a building in the Lisbon earthquake, suffering agony for their last hours of life. No one knows about them, so no one feels compassion; no one makes a heroic attempt to save them. There's just the agony and nothing else — why does God allow it?

More importantly, the argument's moral assumptions are repellent. Compassion for suffering is indeed a virtue, and a world with pain and sympathy for it is better than a world with pain and no sympathy. But the compassion can't be so good that it justifies the pain: a world with pain and sympathy can't be better than a world with no pain at all.

People sometimes argue in ways that deny this. Some neoconservatives attack the welfare state by saying it removes the occasion for private charity. But this argument — that there ought to be poor people so the rich can be generous to them — is morally odious, as is the parallel argument about God. If God made some people suffer so others could sympathize with them, he used the first group as tools to benefit the second — an utterly immoral act.

The world clearly contains evil — there's malice and misery. This isn't surprising if the world evolved naturally, by physical and biological processes. But it can't be squared with the hypothesis of a perfectly good Creator; if you look rationally at the world, you can't be a Christian.

QUESTIONS FOR DISCUSSION

1. What is worse about the world: the moral evil, or sin, it contains or the existence of physical evil, that is, pain?

2. Even if it's true that looking rationally at the world you can't be a Christian, could you nonetheless believe in God non-rationally, by faith?

3. Discuss the argument that the welfare state is bad because it removes the occasion for private charity. Are there circumstances in which this could be a good argument?

Why Littering
Is like Murder

*I*n "Alice's Restaurant," the 1960s folk song by Arlo Guthrie, it was a joke: the U.S. Army had doubts about drafting Mr. Guthrie to kill Vietnamese villagers because he'd once been arrested for littering. But as psychologist Alfie Kohn suggests in *The Brighter Side of Human Nature* (Basic Books), there may be a connection. People who drop cigarette butts or pieces of paper wherever they happen to be show, if to a lesser degree, the same failure of imagination that can let you fire a gun at a stranger.

The essence of moral thinking is realizing that other people's interests matter as much as your own. Things can be good or bad for them just as for you, and just as importantly so. The moral attitude is impartial, counting harms and benefits to oneself no more or less than to other people.

For most of us, adopting this attitude requires empathy. We have to understand our effects on others not just intellectually but emotionally, after imagining them from the inside, as they would feel if they happened to us. This is the point of the Golden Rule, "Do unto others as you would have them do unto you." It gets us to imagine the situations of others as they feel them, with the same detail and intensity.

Even minor wrongdoing involves a failure of this imagination. As Mr. Kohn says, people who litter, double-park, or rip pages out of library books "seem to be locked into themselves, unable or unwilling to consider those who will have to look at their garbage, manoeuvre their cars around them, or discover a chapter missing." Maybe they don't realize what they're doing to others; maybe they do but don't let themselves feel it. Either way, they don't connect empathically with the people they're harming.

It's a long way from littering to killing, but it's down the same road. There, too, you have to ignore emotionally what you're doing to someone—ignore the fear and the loss, to your victim and his or her loved ones.

Fortunately, most of us can't manage this. Killing is too large a harm to sweep under a carpet, especially when the victim is standing in front of us looking human, vulnerable, and afraid.

Consider how wars require propaganda to dehumanize and depersonalize the enemy. Earlier, this propaganda was racial, vilifying Jews, Japs, or the Hun; today it goes for individuals, painting Moammar Gaddafi, Ronald Reagan, or Saddam Hussein as a madman or devil. Either way, it testifies to the power of human empathy: only when an enemy has been dehumanized can we bring ourselves to kill him or her.

Often the propaganda doesn't work. Mr. Kohn cites a striking study of U.S. infantry who fought in the Second World War. At most, 20 or 25 percent had actually fired their weapons in battle. The rest weren't afraid; they regularly faced danger. They just couldn't bring themselves to kill another person.

We should be cheered by this evidence of our altruism, but not to excess, for in smaller cases our empathy often doesn't kick in. Littering, we persuade ourselves, isn't really a harm at all; victims out of sight are too easily out of mind.

It's like what many people saw in the massacre of fourteen women at L'École polytechnique in Montreal in December 1989. Of course the killer, Marc Lepine, was psychologically disturbed, unlike most men. But he differed only in the degree of his refusal to accept women as equals. His act showed the dark side of a common attitude, and also warned where innocent-looking social changes can lead.

Imagine that male attitudes to women are arranged in a bell curve, with the majority around a median of mild sexism and some extremes in either direction. It makes sense that if you move the median in a sexist direction — if you make the majority a little less accepting of women — you'll also move the extremes. What's a small change in most men can push a few over the edge.

So it is with empathy: littering and double-parking show to a lesser degree the same failing present in murder. This is chilling in itself, and also a warning for the future. Many commentators have noted the growing incivility of modern urban life: the impoliteness, the aggression, the bloody-mindedness about small things. This incivility weakens the emotional foundations of moral thinking in all of us; we shouldn't be surprised if, in a few people, it destroys those foundations.

QUESTIONS FOR DISCUSSION

1. Is it true that morality requires us to be impartial, counting benefits and harms to ourselves no more or less than those to other people?

2. Is it psychologically possible to empathize fully with other people, and understand the harms you would cause them, but still choose to litter, double-park, or kill?

3. Are there ways we can increase our empathy, becoming more aware of and sensitive to the effects on others of what we do?

Is There Such a Thing as Moral Luck?

I was bicycling down the main street in Oxford and getting ready to turn right. (This was England, where a right turn is a left turn.) In a hurry, I gave only a quick look back before pulling away from the curb. I didn't see the cyclist behind me, crashed into him, and sent him sprawling into the roadway.

The cyclist was lucky. If there had been a car coming he would have been killed, but there wasn't. He brushed off his clothes, accepted my apology, and continued down the street.

I, too, was lucky. If there had been a car coming, I would have been guilty of carelessly killing someone, a serious moral wrong. As it was, I had been only harmlessly negligent — nothing to be proud of, but no great sin.

But how could luck have the second, excusing effect? How could fortune affect the wrongness of what I did?

A long Western tradition limits moral evaluation to things inside a person's soul, to things he or she controls. It's reflected in Christian attitudes to money. If a rich and a poor person both give to charity, the rich person may give more and do more good. But if the poor person's motives are the same, Christianity says the act is just as worthy.

The same thinking appears in judgements about responsibility. Primitive moralities blame people for things they couldn't prevent, but modern ethics insists on voluntariness. If someone couldn't help what they did—if it was a physical spasm or they were forced—we absolve them of blame.

This tradition expresses a profound moral egalitarianism. Whatever is true of worldly success—of fame, fortune, or happiness—the moral life is something at which everyone has an equal chance. It's a matter of inner states that outside factors, including luck, can't affect.

Although it's inspiring, this tradition isn't one we consistently follow. I learned this on Oxford High Street. If there had been a car coming, I (like anyone in that situation) would have felt terribly guilty. As it was, I shuddered briefly at what might have been and forgot the incident. But why this difference in attitude? In both circumstances my inner states, what I controlled, were the same.

Or consider a feature of our legal system: it punishes attempted crimes, such as attempted murder, less severely than successful ones. This might make sense if the law's purpose were just to prevent future crimes. Stiffer penalties for successful crimes dissuade people who've already tried a crime unsuccessfully from trying it again. But if punishment is a response to guilt, the law is puzzling: why should a gunman be thought less guilty if his victim wore a bulletproof vest?

We seem to believe in "moral luck," in luck that affects not only what happens but also the moral quality of what we do. In the bicycle example, this luck came after my act and determined what its effect would be. But there can also be moral luck in the circumstances and temptations we face.

Imagine that two husbands have equally weak characters and are equally likely to deceive their wives should the opportunity arise. For one the opportunity does arise and he commits adultery; for the other, through no merit of his, it does not. We judge these husbands differently, and so would their wives, for only one has actually deceived. But how fair is this when the other's character is no different, when his more honest behaviour is only the result of moral luck?

There are more chilling examples. In the 1930s, German citizens should have understood Nazism and fought against it. That they didn't means they failed in ways that we in comfortable Canada have not. But can we say honestly that, in those circumstances, we would have acted better? If we can't, can we feel morally superior?

There are different explanations of our belief in moral luck, but the true one is probably cowardice. We haven't the courage to think through moral ideas that imply we can be just as morally flawed when we don't kill or deceive as when we do.

In a great 1960s folk song, Phil Ochs called for this courage: "Show me a prisoner," or a hobo or a drunkard, he sang, "And I'll show you a young man, / With so many reasons why, / There but for fortune may go you or I." The song doesn't deny that what the prisoner did was wrong. It only says that, if we haven't done something similar, it's because of the luck of our social position.

Like many reformers, Mr. Ochs was calling for a return to old moral ideas, in this case the Greek and Christian idea that morality is a matter of the inner life, of states of our soul that we control. It's an idea we'd do well to remember when feeling smug that we've never actually killed, deceived, or connived with Nazis.

QUESTIONS FOR DISCUSSION

1. Should someone who inherits a large fortune feel more proud of their large contributions to charity than a poor person does of their smaller contributions?

2. If we believe that had we lived in Nazi Germany in the 1930s, we would have acted no better than Germans then did, how should we react: by thinking less badly of the Germans or worse of ourselves?

3. Is it unfair if some people are born with a virtuous character while others are born with strong temptations to do evil?

Partial Failure Is Also Partial Success

*W*e were between rounds at our favourite golf course, and ordering lunch. "And a Coke float," George concluded, "but could you make it with Diet Coke?" We hooted with derision. "If you're so concerned about calories, George, why are you eating ice cream?"

We were calling George a hypocrite. There are two honest options, we were saying: be serious about healthy eating and forget the ice cream, or have a float but don't pretend—make it with real Coke.

But why? Why is anything less than the best no better than nothing at all? In our derision we were committing what is sometimes called the "either-or fallacy"—either you do everything possible for healthy eating or what you do has no merit.

Maybe George should have ordered fresh fruit. (Tough to get at a golf course, but let's ignore that.) But if he was having ice cream, wasn't it better to have a drink without sugar? If the issue is your intake of calories, surely some reduction is better than none.

This thinking wouldn't matter if we applied it only to dieting, but we extend it to morality. Either you're a total saint, we say, or you're no better than a total sinner. And that's a dangerous doctrine.

You know the argument. You're protesting something like the killing in El Salvador and someone says, "What about the Soviet invasion of Afghanistan? I don't hear you say anything about that." This isn't a friendly remark, pointing to another topic of potential interest. It disparages the whole issue of Salvadoran killing and, especially, any claim that you're doing something right in addressing it.

Well, there are many evils in the world, and you're not opposing all of them. But there can be many reasons for this. Maybe you agree that Soviet actions in Afghanistan were wrong but haven't time to protest everything. Maybe you think they were right. None of this shows that the Salvadoran killing isn't evil, or that you're not doing one good thing in protesting against it. That you're not opposing all evils doesn't mean you have no right to oppose any.

Or imagine that a businessperson makes large contributions to charity. If we notice that he hasn't given his entire fortune — he still has his BMW and swimming pool — we say, "He's no better than you or I." If he has some questionable motive — he wants more public recognition of his charity than is consistent with true altruism — we think this undercuts all his virtue. If he's not completely good, he may as well be bad.

According to some moral systems, there's a truth this thinking exaggerates. If we ought always to do what's best, then anything less than the best is wrong. But it's a mistake to conclude that all wrongs are equally wrong, or that failing a little is no better than failing entirely.

The effects of either-or thinking depend on who does it. If we were nearly morally perfect, this thinking might be an inspiration. "If I don't do that little extra bit," we might say, "all I've done will count for nothing. So here's a special effort." (Saints may think this way.)

But the problem in our world is hardly that people are a little less than perfect. We're far from saints, and for us either-or thinking becomes an excuse. "If I can't oppose all the world's evils," we tell ourselves, "I may as well not oppose any." "If he's not giving everything to charity, I'll give only a pittance."

And there are worse effects. Our century has seen the replacement of limited war by total war. Where past conflicts were fought by rules forbidding, for instance, the intentional killing of noncombatants, we now accept the obliteration bombing of cities and even threats to annihilate whole populations. This is partly the result of either-or thinking. If war is totally evil, we've been persuaded, there can't be gradations of wrongness among wars. "War is hell," the generals said, and proceeded to make it so.

There are popular sayings that encapsulate this thinking, and we should realize they are false. "In for a penny, in for a pound." Why not in for a shilling and a half? "You may as well be hanged for a sheep as for a lamb." Not the accepted wisdom among sheep. The one who had it right was Voltaire: "The best is the enemy of the good."

The idea isn't to affirm moral laxness, to say we can have moral Coke floats so long as we sweeten them with Aspartame. If we in fact have a duty to do what's best, anything less than that is wrong. But there are more than just the two categories. Some wrongs are less wrong than others; some are even close to rights.

The task in our time isn't to move people the last little distance to moral perfection; it's to encourage those who act badly to act better. To this end we should recognize partial successes as that — partial *successes* — not lump them with all failures. Maybe we'll oppose evils one at a time; let's note that we're opposing some. Maybe we'll give only moderately to charity; that's better than giving nothing.

QUESTIONS FOR DISCUSSION

1. Is it true that we ought always to do what's best, or are there situations where doing what's best, especially for other people, is more than one's duty requires?

2. Is it legitimate to criticize a vegetarian who says killing animals is wrong by pointing out that he or she hasn't publicly protested the killing of humans in, say, the former Yugoslavia?

3. If there are many good causes to which you could contribute, how do you decide among them? Must you give to the most worthy cause (assuming you know what that is), or can you let your tastes and interests decide which cause you'll support?

Part Five

Justice and Economic Distribution

$\mathcal{S}$ome important questions about justice concern the distribution of wealth, income, and opportunities. Should everyone have an equal share of these means to the good life, or should some people have more than others? If the latter, on what basis should some have more? The first three essays in this part examine the consequences of different economic distributions for people's well-being and moral character; the next two introduce considerations of fairness and desert. The last essay discusses a topic of interest to some students: the relationship between students' fields of study at university and their ability to work effectively in business.

Some Taxing
Questions about Wealth

*W*hen the Goods and Services Tax was introduced in Canada it was caught in a crossfire, opposed by both ends of the political spectrum. The political right disliked the GST just because it's a tax, a symbol of government waste and interference. The left had a more complicated objection.

People on the political left don't mind taxes as such; they're happy to pay them if they fund worthwhile social programs. But opponents thought the GST was the wrong kind of tax because it abandons progressivity, the idea that those who earn more should pay at a higher rate.

Income taxes can be and are progressive. Since your tax return records your total income for the year, there can be higher rates for higher earnings. But sales taxes are collected purchase by purchase, with no reference to total income. Under the GST, everyone pays the same 7 percent, although low-income Canadians get a special tax rebate.

Why care about progressivity? Since progressive taxes reduce inequalities in wealth and

income, the question really is: why care about
equality?

The simplest argument for economic equality
is that it's efficient, a good means to what should
be the goal of economic activity.

No one thinks that money is an end in itself.
It's at best a means to what's truly good: happiness, self-direction, achievement. Nor is it always
equally good as a means. There are diminishing
returns from money, or, as economists would say,
there is diminishing marginal utility. The more
dollars you have, the less you benefit from an
extra dollar.

Let's say you're poor, a single mother living on
welfare. An extra thousand dollars will make a
large difference to your quality of life. Now imagine that you're Paul Reichmann. An extra thousand dollars won't get noticed, and even if it does,
won't significantly affect your well-being.

Given this trend, if we have extra funds to dis-
tribute, we do best by giving them to those who
have least. And if we take from the rich to give to
the poor — as we do if we combine progressive
taxation with welfare payments — we do more
good than harm. The losses to the rich are
smaller than the gains to those who started with
less. In fact, the most efficient distribution of
wealth is an exactly equal distribution. It puts
resources where they will be most effective in
providing true benefits.

This is an initial argument for equality, but
there's a counter-argument. If money is good as a
means, we should want the total available to be as
large as possible. And the size of this total is
affected by how it's distributed.

We all know the argument. If society's wealth
is divided equally, no one has a self-interested
reason to work to make it larger. We have to
rely on people's love of others, a notoriously
weak motive. To increase social wealth we need

incentives, higher earnings for those who produce more. These incentives create inequality, but the net result can be better for many and could be better for all. An equal share of the socialist pie could be smaller than the smallest share of a monster capitalist cake.

One idea has led in contrary directions. We want the economy to promote true human goods such as happiness, autonomy, and achievement. This makes us want to make the most efficient use of the wealth we have, which means dividing it equally. But we also want to create wealth, which can require inequality.

The political left and right differ in how they weigh these arguments. The left thinks distribution is more important and favours generous social programs funded by progressive taxes. The right focuses on production, which it pursues even at the cost of inequality.

In the 1980s, the right was politically ascendant. In Britain, the United States, and Canada, the tax system became less progressive. In 1980, our top marginal tax rate was 65 percent; today it is 44 percent.

If flattening tax rates has a justification, it is some version of the trickle-down theory: benefits to the rich stimulate the economy and eventually reach everyone. This may be true. But there's a reason for doubt.

Diminishing marginal utility means that extra wealth does less for you the more you have. If this applies to individuals, it should also apply to societies: the importance of increasing social wealth should lessen as social wealth increases. Canada's per capita GNP is larger today than in 1980, and was larger then than in 1970. As time passes, should we not worry less about growth and more about the optimal use of what we have?

The ultimate goal of economics is moral: to promote whatever is truly good in human lives. It was ancient wisdom that a good life requires some material resources but not a great deal. We could use that wisdom in tax policy today.

QUESTIONS FOR DISCUSSION

1. Is it true that there is diminishing marginal utility from money, so the benefit of an extra dollar gets less the more dollars you have? Or can wealth create new desires and even needs?

2. Are there more radical arguments for economic equality than the one proposed in the essay, arguments that an equal division of wealth is right in itself, is what people deserve, or is required by fairness?

3. In deciding about economic policy today, we should consider the effects on future generations. Would our descendants benefit more from a wealthier economy now or from a more equal distribution now?

Why the Rich Don't Shovel Sidewalks

*M*y sister and brother-in-law live in a fairly flash neighbourhood of Toronto. A visitor out for a late-night stroll can pass by some of the highest-priced real estate in the country.

It makes you wonder: why is it that the richer the neighbourhood and the bigger the house, the less likely it is that the sidewalk in front has been shovelled clear of snow?

In my middle-class neighbourhood, we don't all shovel our walks every snowfall. But on a given winter's day, a half to two-thirds of the sidewalks have been swept meticulously clean. This is less impressive than in a working-class neighbourhood to the west of us, but far better than what I saw outside the mansions of Toronto.

Though it's only five minutes' work, shovelling a sidewalk has social significance.

It is, first, something you do mainly for the comfort and safety of others. In this it's entirely unlike shovelling your driveway, which benefits only you. Are clean sidewalks really important? To a teenager with good boots, probably not. But for a pensioner with an arthritic hip, walking on rough, uneven ground is vastly more painful than walking on a level surface.

In a way, shovelling snow is like gift giving. When it's done, people get not only easy walking but also the pleasure of noticing, even if subconsciously, that someone took the trouble to provide it for them. When it's not done, they have the extra annoyance, of which they usually are conscious, that some jerk couldn't be bothered.

Shovelling can also express community. If you live where most people clean their walks, you can think of your cleaning as part of a communal effort to make the whole neighbourhood hospitable. There has never been a meeting about this; there's no formal plan. But there can be unspoken co-operation among many people to achieve a goal they all value.

There may be many reasons why people in big houses don't clean their walks. Perhaps the snow in their neighbourhoods is heavier than the snow that falls elsewhere. Perhaps they haven't time, being too busy with volunteer work at the local food bank. Or is there something deeper?

A long philosophical tradition says that too much wealth can corrupt your values, turning you away from what really matters, including civility and concern for others, toward more material acquisition.

Plato, designing his ideal city, asks whether its rulers should have private property: "Do you think that a potter who has become wealthy will still be willing to pay attention to his craft?" Assuming the answer is no, Plato denies property to his city's governors.

Aristotle, characteristically, has a more moderate view. He insists, against Plato, that you need some private possessions to lead a valuable life. But you don't want too many. In money making as in other arts there's a too much as well as a too little — too much to maintain a healthy character.

You can see why on this point Plato and Aristotle were congenial to Christianity: "It is easier for a camel to go through the eye of a needle, than for a rich man to enter into the kingdom of God."

Marx had a different worry. He feared the corrupting effects, not of great material comfort, which he hoped would continue under communism, but of inequalities in people's levels of comfort. If some have more possessions than others, this focuses attention on possessions and away from what is truly valuable.

A further worry for Marx was the mechanism that produces these inequalities. A free-market economy, with its emphasis on competition and self-advancement, sets people against each other. Competing as they do in business life, they come to compete generally. The more that people are implicated in this economy, the less sense of community they feel.

These are different ideas about how economic factors can corrupt people's values, and especially diminish their concern for others. The ideas may be complementary. Different corrupting forces may apply to different people, or all may work simultaneously. But all are denied in the dominant political philosophy of our time, liberalism.

Liberalism in its classical form is based on optimism about human beings. It says that if people are left free of government interference in their private lives, they will find and choose the way of life that is best for them. In its laissez-faire economic versions, it says that if people are unfettered in their economic activity, they will first produce consumer goods and then use them to live as is best.

There is no hint in this of corrupting forces, either within the individual (Plato, Aristotle, Christianity) or in social structures (Marx). Instead, there's a faith that people with the means to live well will in fact live well.

It's an inspiring doctrine, liberalism, and a beautiful one. One wishes it were true. But if it were true, wouldn't you find less materialism and more civility where the market was more successful? Wouldn't there be more shovelled sidewalks on the streets of Forest Hill?

QUESTIONS FOR DISCUSSION

1. How does the idea that too much wealth can corrupt your values relate to the thesis of "diminishing marginal utility" discussed in the previous essay?

2. Was Marx right to worry that a free-market economy makes people aggressive, competitive, and less likely to feel a sense of community with each other?

3. Does a free-market economy affect people's values? For example, does advertising affect what people seek and value in their own lives? If so, is the effect good or bad?

A Market Economy
Makes Us Better People

*I*t was a winter's night and I was walking past a restaurant I knew. The maitre d', Fernando, spotted me through the window, waved, and came out for a chat. I wasn't a frequent customer, but when I ate at the restaurant it was partly for the warm atmosphere. Here Fernando was spreading that atmosphere into the street.

I was reminded of the incident when my wife returned from a stay in communist Czechoslovakia. She described how, in state-run restaurants there, the waiters would say there were no places even though every table was empty. (When they learned you were a tourist, who might tip or change currency, they'd change their tune.) In a shoe store she was asked her shoe size. "I don't know the European size, but at home it's 7 $\frac{1}{2}$." "If you're that stupid, how do you expect me to serve you?"

A classical aim of socialism was to improve personal relations. The idea wasn't that capitalists didn't really love their spouses or children. But a market economy was supposed to create barriers to fellowship in the wider community.

One barrier was economic inequality, especially a system of economic classes. People from different classes would feel awkward with each other. There would be arrogance among the rich, and servility or resentment among the poor.

Another barrier was the competitive market structure. In business, people would try to outsell their rivals and drive them out of business. In private life, they would try to outconsume and outpossess. When the economy set people so much against each other, how could they ever come together?

Yet it was in capitalist Canada that a restaurateur risked a chill to greet an occasional customer, while in Czechoslovakia there was a surly refusal to serve. Could the free market make us kinder and gentler?

In some sectors of a market economy, including restaurants and retail, your success depends very much on the service you give. Customers want to be treated with civility and warmth, and take their business to outfits that provide them. (In a survey of Canadians shopping in the United States, 28 percent said their main reason for crossing the border was better service.) In capitalism, there's a reward for service that doesn't exist in state socialism, where your earnings are unaffected by the number of customers you attract.

Of course, you might give service without really caring about your customers. You could wear a friendly mask that you drop the minute you're out of their sight. But I doubt many people could keep up the act that consistently, and I also suspect we'd see through it. To serve convincingly, you have to want to serve for its own sake.

A businessman at a meeting I recently attended generalized this idea. He said making money is one of the things you can't do by trying to do it. You have to aim at something else, such as filling people's needs, and let profits come as a by-product.

If this is right, the rewards in capitalism can't influence your conscious reasoning. You can't say, "I'll make more money if I value service as an end," because that values service as a means. But the incentives can work indirectly.

One way is by natural selection: only those who care about serving stay in business. Fernando has been successful in his restaurant partly because of his personality; Basil Fawlty would go broke in a week.

The other way is by psychological reinforcement. When you do something nice for a customer, you get more business, and even if you don't notice the connection, this makes you more likely to be nice the next time. When you're rude, you're penalized.

And the reinforcement can spread beyond your business life. The socialist argument assumed that your work experiences can affect your attitude to people generally, and the same seems right here. What makes you want to help customers can make you helpful to all.

Of course, the picture won't be simple. Capitalism has many sides, and if some improve human relationships others make them worse. I doubt that junk bonds or beer ads did anything positive for anyone's character.

Still, there's something in a market economy that encourages altruism and isn't found in state socialism. You may not be aware of it, but it's working behind your back to make you a better person.

QUESTIONS FOR DISCUSSION

1. Is it right to evaluate economic systems, as this essay and the previous one do, by considering their effects on people's characters, or is that an irrelevant consideration?

2. Where the previous essay argues that a competitive free-market economy makes people's characters worse, this one argues that it can make them kinder and gentler. Which argument is more persuasive?

3. Is the essay right that people serving customers can't usually fake it, but must really care about service for its own sake if they're to please their customers? Or is it easier than the essay assumes to put on a friendly mask while remaining essentially self-interested underneath?

Is It Wrong to Cheat on Your Income Tax If Everyone Else Does?

*A*t income tax time, people across the country cheat. Not in a big way, perhaps, but in little things: they hide some income or claim meals with their friends as business expenses. They pay less than they should by the letter of the law.

There's some unfairness here. Many Canadians, especially low-income Canadians, can't cheat on taxes. Their incomes come entirely in wages reported on their T4 slips, and they aren't allowed any business deductions. But let's ignore this and assume that everyone has some latitude for cheating. If they all cheat, is it wrong for you to cheat?

One moral reason to pay taxes is to finance government programs that benefit everyone. But this can't be the decisive moral reason. You'd do even more good if you paid more than your legal share of taxes, yet not doing that isn't the same as cheating.

The main reason to pay is that it's the law, and there's a general obligation to obey the law. Sometimes this obligation makes no moral difference: you ought not to murder whether there's a law against it or not. But sometimes it tips the balance, making morally required what would otherwise be optional. So it seems to be with taxes. Without a tax law, paying would be nice; with a law, it's mandatory.

But what *is* the law about taxes? According to a theory called "legal realism," the law isn't just words on paper, it's a complex institution involving the police, courts, and prisons. The real law is only what this whole institution enforces.

On a city street the posted speed limit may be 50 km/h, but the police arrest only drivers going over 55. If so, legal realists say, the real speed limit is 55. If you drive 54 you aren't breaking the law, you're obeying it.

Tax law seems to work like traffic law. Revenue Canada goes after the big cheaters but lets the little stuff go. So is the little stuff really illegal? In her book *Behind Closed Doors*, Linda McQuaig reports that Mickey Cohen, architect of much tax law in the 1970s, believed in giving taxpayers "breathing space," so they could feel they'd "gotten away with a bit." If you do what the lawmakers want you to, how do you violate their rules?

Maybe legal realism is wrong and the law is just what's written on paper. Even so, we need to know who the obligation to obey the law is owed to and where it comes from.

The most sensible view is that the obligation is owed not to the government, but to your fellow citizens. They've restrained their self-interest by supporting a system that benefits everyone, including you, and it would be unfair if you didn't do the same. You do your share because they've done theirs.

But on income tax they haven't done their share, at least not entirely. Since they're all cheating, you can't owe it to them not to cheat. In fact, if you didn't cheat it would be you who was treated unfairly.

It's not that all cheating is okay. If there was a time when nobody cheated, the people who started cheating acted wrongly. The same goes for people who, when others are cheating a little, cheat a lot. But if everyone cheats a little, no one violates an obligation.

Nor is the amount of cheating in Canada something to be pleased about. For one thing, it's not universal: those whose incomes are all in wages can't participate. (Should they get a special tax credit, as compensation?) And the practice has a built-in tendency to escalate. People who've cheated a little decide other people are cheating more and cheat more themselves, which causes other people to cheat more, and so on. The system can run out of control.

This is a reason to want Revenue Canada to crack down on cheating. If more people pay the full amount, we'll feel a stronger obligation to do the same. It's also a reason to hope this essay won't be read by someone in the middle of doing their tax return.

QUESTIONS FOR DISCUSSION

1. What's the main reason why you ought, ethically, to pay your taxes?

2. If you believe the tax system is unfair, because it taxes you too much or the rich too little, do

you still have an ethical duty to pay your taxes?

3. We wouldn't say that if other people aren't saving a drowning person that makes it right for you not to save the person. Why then say that if others aren't paying their full taxes you needn't pay your full taxes?

If Scrooge Had Been a Nicer Person, He Would Have Gone Bust

*H*e has become as much a part of Christmas as mangers and mistletoe, with his "Bah! Humbug!"; his ghosts of Christmas past, present, and to come; and his moral reform on Christmas Eve. But what is Ebenezer Scrooge's message?

At the start of Charles Dickens's *A Christmas Carol*, Scrooge's character is nasty and his clerk Bob Cratchit is poor. The first is the cause of the second: it is Scrooge's miserliness that keeps the Cratchits needy. A day later, Scrooge is reformed and Cratchit's lot has improved: he has a pay raise, there's coal to warm his office, and his crippled son Tiny Tim will live.

As George Orwell said in a famous essay, the ideas behind this story are naïve. Dickens saw the terrible poverty in England of the 1840s; one of his main aims in writing *A Christmas Carol* was to bring it to his readers' attention. But he thought addressing this poverty didn't require any changes in the economic system, in politics, or in the distribution of power; all that was needed was for people to be nicer. The rich could stay rich, they just had to adopt the Christmas spirit and spread it through the year.

The reformed Scrooge is a common character in Dickens, what Orwell called the Good Rich Man, "a superhumanly kind-hearted old gentleman who 'trots' to and fro, raising his employees' wages, patting children on the head, getting debtors out of jail and, in general, acting the fairy godmother." He's also a "pure dream figure."

The complaint isn't that Dickens isn't a socialist, that at the end of the day Scrooge is still a capitalist and Cratchit still a clerk. It's that Dickens doesn't see the vital influence of social institutions on behaviour. Charity is lovely and a good character always a blessing. But often how you act depends less on what you want than on what the social structure lets you do.

Consider the economics of the firm of Scrooge and Marley. As of Boxing Day, Scrooge has raised Cratchit's wage and will presumably do the same for his other employees. (These are never mentioned, but Scrooge can't have got rich from a two-person operation.) But if the firm's competitors don't raise their wages, Scrooge and Marley will be undersold in the market, will lose profits, and may eventually go bankrupt.

Wages weren't low in the 1840s because employers who could have paid more were stingy. They were low because a competitive market kept them low, because no one who paid more would long remain in business.

Workers are better off today, but this hasn't been the doing of Good Rich Men. As the economy grew, workers were in a stronger bargaining position for wages; they strengthened that position further by forming trade unions (Dickens despised unions); and legislatures passed minimum-wage laws (Dickens scorned politics).

These laws not only forced employers to raise wages but ensured that in doing so, they wouldn't be disadvantaged against their rivals. Economic structures don't just have bad effects such as poverty, they also have good ones. The free-market economy Dickens saw developing has proved remarkably successful at producing consumer goods. This isn't because people living in this economy want especially to make things efficiently; they haven't all been visited by a ghost of productivity to come. The system forces them to be efficient. If they don't constantly strive to increase productivity, they'll fall behind their rivals that do.

Over the last century, the world has groped to find an economic system that both is productive and avoids extreme inequalities in wealth. (Centrally planned socialism fails the first test, laissez-faire capitalism the second.) We've by no means succeeded. But we've rightly been concerned with the institutional structures within which people live.

Dickens's message is that this is a mistake: we should ignore economics, sociology, and political science, and concentrate on individual psychology, on the reform of individual character. A good will is all that matters because it will triumph in any conditions. That's a naïve and dangerous message for Christmas or any other season.

QUESTIONS FOR DISCUSSION

1. How good can Scrooge really be if he retains exclusive control of his company and keeps Bob Cratchit as his clerk, albeit a better paid one?

2. How can a system "force" people to pay low wages or to keep increasing their productivity? Must anything be true about their motives for this forcing to occur?

3. How much better could our society become if, without any change in the social structure, people decided to improve their moral characters?

How to Get to the Top: Study Philosophy

*H*ow should Canada educate students to compete successfully in the business world? Some provincial governments think it is by teaching them business.

In 1990, the Alberta government announced plans for an "unprecedented" expansion of business education at its three universities. Soon after, 120 extra students were studying management at the University of Calgary.

Recent evidence suggests this approach is mistaken. We will produce better managers if we educate them first in traditional subjects in the arts and sciences. We may do best of all if we educate them in philosophy.

Each year, thousands of undergraduates write admissions tests for the prestigious graduate programs. There's the Law School Admission Test (LSAT), the Graduate Management Admission Test (GMAT) for business study, and the Graduate Record Examination (GRE) for other fields. A 1985 study for the U.S. Department of Education compared tests of students from different disciplines, with surprising results.

Consider the GMAT, used for admission to MBA programs and, ultimately, to the highest levels of management. Undergraduate business students, who you'd think would be especially well prepared for this test, do badly on it, scoring below the average for all test takers. The best results are by math students, followed by philosophy students and engineers.

This is typical. Business students score below average on almost all the tests, as do, excepting engineers, all other students in applied or occupational fields. The best results come from students in the natural sciences and humanities. The study concludes that, on tests measuring aptitude for advanced professional study, "undergraduates who major in professional and occupational fields consistently *underperform* those who major in traditional arts and science fields."

The most consistent performers are philosophy students. They are first out of 28 disciplines on one test, second on another, and third on a third. On their weakest test they are still 4.6 percent above the average, the best performance on a weakest test of any group.

Though data here are less consistent, the superior performance of arts and science students continues after university. According to a book by sociologist Michael Useem, they have more difficulty finding beginning managerial jobs than those with business or professional degrees because they lack specific skills in finance or engineering. When they are hired, it is usually lower in the company hierarchy. Once hired, however, they advance more rapidly than their colleagues.

On average, arts and science graduates end their careers level with business and engineering graduates, having closed the gap between them. In some companies with less of an engineering or

MBA "culture," they pass them. An AT&T study showed that, after 20 years with the company, 43 percent of liberal arts graduates had reached upper-middle management, compared with 32 percent of business majors and 23 percent of engineers. The Chase Manhattan Bank found that 60 percent of its worst managers had MBAs while 60 percent of its best managers had BAs. At IBM, nine of the company's top thirteen executives had liberal arts degrees.

What explains the success of arts and science students? Many arguments for liberal education cite a contemporary cliché — that we live in a time of unprecedented change. If the world is in flux, an applied education will soon be out of date. Better the breadth and flexibility given by general studies.

A better explanation points to what cannot change: the basic elements of reasoning and problem solving. The study of admissions tests found that students do best "who major in a field characterized by formal thought, structural relationships, abstract models, symbolic languages, and deductive reasoning." The more abstract a subject, the more it develops pure reasoning skills; and the stronger a person's reasoning skills, the better she'll do in any applied field.

This fits the data from business. Corporations report that, although technical skills are most important in low-level managerial jobs, they become less so in middle and top jobs, where the key traits include communications skills, the ability to formulate problems, and reasoning skills. Liberal arts education may be weak in the prerequisites for beginning managerial jobs but provides just what's needed for success at the top.

This doesn't mean there's no place for business education. Canadian industry needs specialized business skills, and our universities should supply them. But in the increasingly competitive world economy, there will be a premium on vision, creativity, and analytical power, traits better fostered by liberal education.

This points to the recommendation now heard most from chief executive officers: first an arts and science degree in a field like English, physics, or philosophy, then an MBA. First some general intellectual skills, then the specific knowledge needed to apply them in business.

So, to train successful business leaders, Canada should strengthen education in the arts and sciences. And this will have another effect. Students educated in the liberal arts will be more rounded individuals, knowing more about the natural world or the history of their culture and better at reasoning about morality and politics: at the very least, a nice side effect.

QUESTIONS FOR DISCUSSION

1. If philosophy students do better on average on the GMAT test, does this prove that studying philosophy causes you to do better on the test?

2. If philosophy students do better on average on the GMAT test, does this prove that studying philosophy causes you to do better in business?

3. Is something wrong in a business system where the qualities needed for success in getting a first job are different from those needed for promotion to a top job? Can you imagine reforms to business that would correct this situation?

Part Six

The Good Life

*E*thics isn't only about what's right and wrong. It's also about what's good and bad — what's worth living for, or worth promoting in one's own life and others'. The essays in this part take a consistent line about the good. They reject hedonism, the theory that only pleasure is good, and defend the "perfectionist" view that some things are good regardless of how much people want or enjoy them. And they hold that many things are good: knowledge, but not only knowledge; achievements of many kinds, in science, sports, and business; some kinds of fame; and, when it's possible, a well-rounded life. Not all activities are good; some are worthless. But many pursuits have value, suited to the many different talents different people have.

Pleasure Alone Won't Make You Happy

*S*ome people think human beings want only pleasure. Some think we *should* want only pleasure. These people would love the experience machine.

The experience machine is a philosopher's machine, which means it doesn't exist. (It was invented by American philosopher Robert Nozick.) By neural stimulation it can give you any experience or inner feeling you like — of writing a great novel, of scoring a Stanley Cup–winning goal, of deep and passionate love.

You decide in advance what experiences you'd like to have (there's a menu if you're unimaginative), electrodes are attached to your brain, and you then have all the thoughts and feelings associated with your chosen activity. It's exactly as if you were writing that novel or scoring that goal.

Imagine that the experience machine is available and you can go on it for the rest of your life. (Although philosophers' machines don't exist, you have to pretend they do.) Do you want to go on the machine? Will it make your life best to go on it?

If pleasure is all that matters, the answer should be yes, since the machine gives you all the pleasure you can want. It gives you physical pleasure and, if more refined pleasures go with activities like novel writing, it gives you those too.

Yet most of us wouldn't go on the machine. This isn't just a matter of taste, like not liking Chinese food. We think that if we did want to go on the machine we'd be wrong, we'd be wanting what isn't in fact the best life.

Some minor reasons for this should be set aside. We may think going on the machine would be immoral, because it would mean neglecting our duties to others. So imagine that others don't need us, being already well off. Or we may worry that we'll program the machine badly and get stuck in some juvenile fantasy of sex on a desert island. So imagine that we come off the machine every few years to reprogram it. (When we plug back in we forget the reprogramming and become absorbed in our new fantasy.)

Even with these changes, most of us wouldn't go on the machine. This shows something deep about our values.

What exactly is missing on the experience machine? People who plug in are detached from reality. They lack connections to the world around them, in two vital respects.

First, they lack knowledge of their surroundings. When you have knowledge, the way you think the world is corresponds to the way it really is. There's a relation of matching between the thoughts in your mind and the world outside it, and this matching is missing on the experience machine. People think they're writing a novel or playing hockey, but they're not.

Second, people on the machine don't achieve anything. In successful action, you form a goal and transfer it to reality, so the world comes to match an idea in your mind. This, too, is missing on the machine. People intend to write novels or score goals, but their aims are never realized.

As the experience machine shows, we don't care just about pleasure or the quality of our inner experience. We want that experience connected to something outside it. There are real-life illustrations of this.

If you believe your spouse is faithful when he or she isn't, you can have the same feelings as if your spouse were faithful; thus, you can have the same pleasure. But surely being mistaken about such a vital aspect of your life is bad.

Or you may die in the contented belief that you've achieved some important goal. If pleasure were all that matters, the fact that you haven't achieved this goal — yours isn't the cure for cancer — wouldn't harm you. But surely it's a loss.

This doesn't mean that pleasure has no value. Although not the only good thing, it can still be one good thing among others. If we had the experience machine, it might be nice to plug in for five or ten minutes a night. (TV may be a poor person's experience machine.) What wouldn't be good for a whole life can be good for bits of it.

More important, pleasure is a valuable addition to other good things. Knowledge or achievement plus pleasure in them is better than knowledge or achievement alone.

Imagine that a scientist with a profound knowledge of nature takes no pleasure in that knowledge, feeling no excitement about it. We'd think there's something wrong with this scientist. If she doesn't respond positively to her knowledge, her life has less value than it might. Likewise, if we learned that Margaret Atwood gets no pleasure from her novels or Wayne Gretzky doesn't like hockey — he plays just as a job — we'd be troubled. To have its full value, achievement must be joined by a proper pleasure in it.

Pleasure on its own, as on the experience machine, has little value. But when added to other good things it makes them better. In Aristotle's words, pleasure is like "the bloom of youth on those in the flower of their age." Or we might say, it's the icing on the cake.

QUESTIONS FOR DISCUSSION

1. If you *wanted* to spend your life on the experience machine, knowing fully what that involved, would your doing so then be good, or would it still be a waste of your potential?

2. Why should we care about being connected to the world by true beliefs and successful intentions?

3. What does it mean to say that pleasure is the "icing on the cake"?

Was Socrates Right that Philosophy Is the Ultimate Pursuit?

*I*s the unexamined life not worth living? Socrates thought so, or at least he said so at his trial in Athens. But his idea needs examining itself, to see if it's true.

By the examined life, Socrates, doesn't mean the life of psychological self-analysis. He means the philosophical life, devoted to philosophical questions about what's ultimately good. He's telling the court why banishment is unacceptable to him as a punishment: it would mean giving up philosophical conversation with his friends, which he's not prepared to do. And this isn't just a matter of personal taste. Discussing goodness and related topics is "the very best thing a human being can do," and without it no life is worth living.

It sounds fishy: a philosopher philosophizing that philosophy is the best or only good activity. (Does anyone else do this? Singers sing about how great their style of music is—"It don't mean a thing if it ain't got that swing," "It's gotta be rock'n'roll music"—but that's got a beat and you can dance to it.) In Socrates's case, we shouldn't be persuaded.

Let's grant for argument's sake that the best life is an intellectual life. Why does it have to focus on philosophy rather than physics, medicine, or history? In these fields, too, you can stretch your intellectual powers and arrive at integrated, explanatory knowledge. In fact, knowledge seems more likely here than on the hazy topics of philosophy.

Nor is there any reason to confine what's good to the intellect. Lives of action—the athlete's, politician's, or entrepreneur's—also develop human capacities, and in a similar way. The physicist knows a general law that explains many particular facts; the politician has a major goal that requires many different means.

So philosophy isn't uniquely good; a life devoted to something else can be worth living. But maybe a milder version of Socrates's idea is true.

Many activities, this milder view says, can be good. But they're only so when you understand why they're good and choose them for that reason: because you appreciate their goodness.

This is like an idea of the German philosopher Immanuel Kant's: that a morally right action only has moral worth when it's done because it's right. Helping someone because of a feeling, such as sympathy or a desire to ease their pain, is valueless. Only if you're motivated by the stern thought of duty is your action any good.

Most philosophers think this idea is too harsh. There are better and worse motives, but surely sympathy, love, and fellow-feeling are on the good side, not the bad. They're worthy impulses to action, not empty ones.

We should take a similar line with Socrates. Imagine that someone goes for physics, hockey, or entrepreneurship just because they love it for itself, without any fancy thoughts about goodness. Surely this is a better motive than if they did it just to make money or to impress other people. And surely it's enough to make their activity good: doing something potentially valuable out of love makes it actually valuable.

It doesn't follow that philosophy is worthless, or that the examined life is not worth living. Philosophy remains one good activity among many, and it can make any other activity better. Doing physics or hockey out of love *and* because you appreciate its goodness is better than doing it just out of love: it adds another worthy motive.

It's a common exaggeration: taking one good thing and saying it's the best or only good thing. (Some tunes without swing do mean a thing; it doesn't have to be rock'n'roll music.) We should forgive Socrates for overdoing his praise of philosophy. In fact, we should see it as a sign of something wonderful. Socrates exaggerated about philosophy because he loved it so deeply, and that love helped make his pursuit of it such a splendid human achievement.

QUESTIONS FOR DISCUSSION

1. Could Socrates argue that every life should contain *some* philosophy, that is, some understanding of what makes other activities good?

2. Is there one kind of life that is best for everyone, or can many different lives be good, so that people must choose among them by seeing which best suits their talents and situation?

3. If someone does physics or plays hockey only to make money, does that make their activity less valuable than if they did the same thing partly for its own sake?

Where There's a Will, There's No Way

"*W*here there's a will, there's a way." Like many snappy proverbs, this one is often false. Many good things can't be had by those who try to get them, only by those who don't.

Our modern age is marked by willfulness. We believe that if something is worth having, we should make getting it our goal, form a plan for achieving this, and carry through the plan. This has been the assumption of self-help manuals from *The Sensuous Man* to *The One-Minute Manager*.

It was a piece of ancient wisdom that this willfulness is often self-defeating. The ancient hedonists thought pleasure was the only good thing but knew that pleasure can often be found only by looking for something else.

Take the pleasure of playing hockey. I can't get this pleasure if, while playing, I constantly think about it. If, crossing the blueline, I ask myself, "Will I get more pleasure passing the puck to Frank or shooting?" I won't get much pleasure at all. For that I have to aim at something else, such

as winning or just playing well, and let my enjoyment come through it.

What's true on the hockey rink is also true for
bigger pleasures. Mother Teresa seems a serene,
happy person. But if she is happy, it's because she
doesn't care much about her own happiness. Her
goals are outside herself: in helping others or
doing the will of God. If she thought more about
her own happiness she would have less of it.

Philosophers call this "the paradox of hedonism," but the phenomenon is quite general. The
Norwegian writer Jon Elster speaks generally of
"states that are essentially by-products" — states
that can't be achieved by aiming at them, but only
as a by-product of aiming at something else.

Take respect, especially respect for being
strong and self-sufficient. If I try to win this
respect from you, I show that I care about your
respect, which shows that I'm not strong and self-
sufficient. Paradoxically, respect goes only to
those who are indifferent to it.

(Pierre Trudeau was always respected, even by
those who hated him, in part because he didn't
care whether anyone respected him. Brian
Mulroney will never be respected, because he so
evidently craves it.)

Love is more complicated. Sometimes my
desire for your desire will inflame your desire. But
sometimes love involves respect, and then my
wanting your love too much, especially my wanting it in too whining a way, may mean that I
never get it. If you're like Groucho Marx, you
won't want to join a club so eager to have you as a
member.

Even when we have love, we try using our wills
to sustain it. If a marriage or love affair is going
badly, we think the thing to do is sit down, discuss what is wrong, and draw up a plan for correcting it. Sometimes this is helpful, even vital.
But sometimes, when what's needed is a return to

spontaneous, natural interaction, more planning will do more harm than good.

There are other areas where our wills defeat us. Psychiatrist Leslie H. Farber says we "can will knowledge, but not wisdom; going to bed, but not sleeping; eating, but not hunger; meekness, but not humility; scrupulosity, but not virtue; self-assertion or bravado, but not courage; lust, but not love." A nice list, though Farber is obviously wrong about lust.

What can we do about our willfulness? By aiming directly at happiness, respect, and other good things, we end up with less of them. Can we change our ways?

Unfortunately, the state of not willing what can't be willed is itself a state that can't be willed. Commanding yourself to stop caring about your own happiness or to stop wanting others to respect you won't work. The ancient wisdom seems of least use to those who most need it.

But the situation isn't entirely bleak. Sometimes states that can't be willed directly can be brought about indirectly. We can place ourselves in situations where, through time, our motives will change. This leads to some advice for those Canadian cities now striving to be, yes, "world class."

It's part of being world class that one doesn't care or at least worry about being world class. Look at Parisians, for example. Do they say, "We're a world-class city because we've got a world-class baseball stadium?" They only think about other cities when wondering idly which one or two might be half as good as theirs.

Because of this, the attempt to become world class, even the declaration that one is, is conclusive proof that one is not.

So Canadian cities should, first, be quiet about being world class. Then they should ask themselves: what projects would we pursue and what buildings would we build if no one else were watching and we had to choose them just for their own sakes?

Having answered this question, they should proceed with those projects and buildings. If they do, they may come to love the projects just for their own sakes, and if that happens, they may actually become world class. For cities, as for individuals, where there's a will, there often isn't a way. Where there isn't a will, there may just be a way.

QUESTIONS FOR DISCUSSION

1. What attitudes lie behind the assumption that all good things can be got by trying to get them? Does anything about our modern societies encourage these attitudes?

2. If a marriage or love affair is going badly, how often is it helpful to discuss the problem and make a plan for solving it, and how often is this approach counter-productive?

3. If I plan to get you to love me and my plan succeeds, should I think less of you and your love than if you fell in love with me without my having planned it?

The Alluring Contours of a Well-Rounded Life

*T*he 1980s were the decade for having it all: the career, the family, the Mercedes, the travel, the windsurfing, and, every six months, some quality time with dear friends. It was a time for Renaissance or, if you like, dim sum lives, given to a little taste of everything.

Now, well into the 1990s, we can be sceptical. Isn't there a saying about being a jack of all trades and a master of none? May the flip side of well-roundedness not be dilettantism?

There's certainly something appealing about a well-rounded life. There are many human excellences, and it's better to have a balanced achievement of them all than to be narrowly specialized on one. It gives your life an intrinsically desirable shape.

This means the excellences have different values for different people. Let's say you're a businessperson who's always been a doer, not a thinker: you've accomplished many goals but haven't thought much about yourself or the world. To balance your life, it's more important for you to gain some understanding than to make another deal. But for intellectuals the priority is reversed. It's more important for them to do something active than to have more ideas.

Other things being equal, then, we should prefer the excellences we've neglected. But when are other things equal? We want not just many excellences, but substantial achievements in what we do. What's the effect on this of a search for well-roundedness?

Initially, the effect is bad. In many fields you have to invest considerable time before anything valuable results. In a science there are basic concepts to learn, in a practice there are fundamental skills, and without them your activity counts for little. (Think of learning a language: without a grasp of the grammar, individual bits of vocabulary don't mean much.) If you try so many activities that you never master any fundamentals, you waste yourself.

Further along, you can often gain more from an activity the more you've put into it. Once you have the basic concepts or skills you can use them to acquire new ones, and your progress speeds up. You accomplish more where you've done more before.

These facts undercut the ideal of well-roundedness. In itself it's more important for the businessperson to think and for the intellectual to do, but the switching is hard. If they both read a philosophy book, the businessperson will learn less, lacking the background to read it critically. If they both run a company, the intellectual will go broke.

If these were the only relevant facts, the best life might be narrowly specialized on one activity. But at higher levels of achievement, there are effects on the other side.

If you do only one activity, chances are you'll get tired or bored. You'll miss the invigorating effect of variety, as well as the chance to enrich yourself in one area with experiences gained doing something different. Major scientific advances often occur when insights from one field are applied to another, and the same holds generally. To do your best at one activity you need familiarity with some others.

This at least moderates our conclusion. It's still wrong to be a pure all-rounder, but it's also wrong to be a pure specialist. Not only does this move you further from an ideal of well-roundedness, but it limits you in your specialty. For most people the best life is somewhat specialized, concentrating moderately on a few activities — not a jack of all trades, but a master of one or two and a jack of a couple.

What does this mean for the 1990s? For many of us it means cutting back. Keep the career (maybe) and the family, but think hard about the rest. Friendships require work, as does a golf swing. You can't learn much from Paris if you stay just a weekend. It's time for some choosing.

It's an inspiring ideal: a well-rounded life with high achievements in many fields. A few individuals with unusual talents — Leonardo da Vinci, Marcus Aurelius — can realistically pursue it. Those of us with more modest gifts must content ourselves with being some kind of specialist.

QUESTIONS FOR DISCUSSION

1. Why is the ideal of a well-rounded life attractive? Is there a competing ideal of a completely specialized life, one whose achievements in its best field are as great as they can possibly be?

2. How should we evaluate the life of a dilet-
tante, someone who tries many activities but
never accomplishes much in any one?

3. What does this essay imply about how university students should choose the courses they
take in a four-year degree?

Pleasure Is Fleeting, but Achievements Live On

*I*magine waking up in hospital one morning with no memory of what happened in the past 24 hours. You were admitted two days ago for an operation that is extremely painful and can't be done with anesthetics. To make up for this a little, the doctors usually induce short-term amnesia in patients after the operation. You wonder, "Was I operated on yesterday?"

You ask a nurse, but she can't remember the exact details of your case: "You're either a patient who had a very long operation yesterday — the most painful we've ever performed — or a different patient who will have a short operation today." She goes off to see which one you are.

As you await the news, what do you hope? English philosopher Derek Parfit, who devised the example, thinks you'll hope fervently that you're the first patient, whose operation is over. You'll prefer to have more pain in your life, so long as the pain is in your past.

Your reaction shows something important about rationality. According to a common theory, being rational involves caring equally about all the times in your life. You're irrational if, for example, you care more about the present than about the future, and knowingly choose small short-term benefits at the cost of larger long-term harms.

But in the example above you can't care equally about *all* times, if that includes times in the past. That would mean hoping that you're the second patient, whose pain is yet to come.

The same holds true for pleasure. Would you rather learn that you won a big lottery ten years ago but blew the money having a good time or that you will win a small lottery this year? Surely you'd rather have your pleasure ahead of you.

These reactions are so natural that our thinking about rationality has to accommodate them. Maybe we ought to care equally about pains and pleasures in the present and future, but we needn't care at all about those in our past.

Interestingly, this accommodation isn't needed for other things we often think are good, for example, achievements.

Imagine waking up in hospital with temporary amnesia and being told that you're either a scientist who made a major discovery last year or a different scientist who will make a minor discovery next year. Surely you'll hope you're the first scientist: you'll want your life to contain the greatest scientific achievement possible, regardless of when it occurs. Unlike past pleasures and pains, past achievements and failures continue to matter to us. The best things we've done can still make us feel proud; the worst can make us cringe.

This difference has implications for our fear of impending death. By this fear I don't mean an abstract regret that you aren't immortal or won't live long enough to try several careers. I mean the fear of death as something that's approaching, coming closer in time, a fear that's strongest when death is most imminent.

I assume that death is just non-existence. There's no heaven or hell, just the dissolution of the body and, with it, the dissolution of you. Because of this, death isn't positively bad, like pain. And there are ways of being alive that are worse than death, for example, intense suffering. Still, death involves the absence of anything good, forever. It's infinite nothingness.

What you fear when death approaches is the fact that you'll never exist again. But on the other side, it will always be true that you *did* exist. It will always be true that you lived the life you did, with its specific experiences and activities. Is this some consolation?

The answer depends on how you lived. If you lived only for pleasure, your past can be of little comfort. Feelings that are gone count for nothing today (remember the old lottery win). You have emptiness ahead of you and nothing substantial behind you.

But past achievements do matter today (remember the old scientific discovery). If you lived for them, you have a counterweight to the nothingness ahead. Whatever comes, it will always be true that you did that research, helped those people, or founded that business. It's there forever, a life that mattered then and matters now. Looking back, you can say, as in the Gershwins' song, "They can't take that away from me."

QUESTIONS FOR DISCUSSION

1. Does the essay accurately describe your reactions in the two main examples: would you prefer more pain so long as it was in your past but also prefer to be the scientist with the major discovery last year?

2. What is the difference between an "abstract regret that you aren't immortal" and the "fear of death as something that's approaching"?

3. How much can memories of what your past life contained console you in the face of impending death?

Part Seven

Equality and Discrimination

*E*quality and non-discrimination are prominent modern ideals; racism and sexism are widely decried as evil. But although it's often clear what non-discrimination requires, for example, that all races have the vote, at other times it's not so clear. Is it wrong to discriminate in one's private life, for example, in whom one invites to dinner? If not, how far does one's "private life" extend? Is it wrong to make hiring decisions using statistical information about racial or gender groups, or to discriminate in favour of the disadvantaged, as in affirmative action? Settling these issues requires some hard thinking about what, exactly, equality requires.

Affirmative Action: Giving Women an Even Break at Work

*I*n the United States, important social policies are mandated by the courts and become the subjects of intense political controversy. In Canada, they get introduced by bureaucrats against only mild murmurs of protest.

So it was when affirmative action (a.k.a reverse discrimination) crossed the border and took up Canadian residence under the name "employment equity."

Affirmative action means giving preference in hiring, promotion, or university admission to members of disadvantaged groups. In Canada, the selected groups are women, Natives, visible minorities, and the employable handicapped.

Administratively, affirmative action can take three forms. The mildest is a tie-breaking scheme. If two candidates are judged to be equally well qualified, you prefer, say, the woman to the man. Next is an extra-points scheme. A candidate gets extra credit, over and above her normal qualifications, for being a woman. This means she can be hired ahead of a man who would otherwise be judged more qualified. Finally, there are quotas. Certain places are set aside for women, and men cannot compete for them.

Opponents of affirmative action often say they don't mind tie breaking; supporters loudly deny they favour quotas. But in fact, these administrative differences are morally trivial. The important question is: what morally justifies any affirmative action?

Here the move across the border has made a difference.

U.S. discussions assume that affirmative action means hiring someone who is in a traditional sense less qualified — that is, who will do less well in the job on a day-to-day basis. But the official Canadian line is that affirmative action is needed to ensure that the most qualified person *is* hired, that "systemic" barriers don't prevent talented women from advancing as they should.

Isn't this contradictory? How can telling managers *not* to hire the most qualified person help them to hire the most qualified?

The objection assumes that the candidate managers *think* is most qualified is *in fact* most qualified. This is often not so.

Affirmative action began in the federal civil service when it was found that, although women held 40 percent of civil service jobs, they had only 5 percent of the top jobs. Faced with this statistic, no one could pretend that civil service promotions were based on actual merit. Civil service managers were preferring less qualified men to more qualified women.

One reason for this could be conscious sexism, the conscious belief that women are inferior or should not have important jobs. Though once common, this is less so now.

More persistent is subconscious sexism, or the subconscious use of sexist stereotypes. Someone who believes himself free of prejudice may have a subconscious picture of women as inferior that he applies to women candidates and that makes him find them less qualified.

Or the cause may be more innocent. Even if men and women can do some jobs equally well, they may do them differently, using different talents and personal strengths. But if only men have had the job before, managers may think the male way of doing it is the only way. They may, honestly and understandably, not count as qualifications female traits that haven't been able to show they're qualifications.

These factors can be pervasive and enduring. When they exist — and the statistics show they often exist — there is a morally uncontestable case for affirmative action.

Given the factors, if managers think a woman is equally or nearly equally qualified with a man, she is probably more qualified. This justifies tie breaking and extra points. If a candidate is rated among the best women, she is probably among the best, period. This can justify quotas.

Deciding exactly how many extra points to give or what quotas to use requires estimating the percentage of women who would be hired if actual merit were decisive. This is a controversial matter, about which honest people can disagree. But if we allow that managers can misrate candidates, we can justify some affirmative action without giving up the traditional idea that hiring should be by merit.

We can't, however, justify all the affirmative action that has been proposed in Canada.

Imagine there's a job you think should be filled 50 percent by women, but that now has only 20 percent women. If you use the official Canadian argument, you can now start hiring at a rate of 50 percent women. But then the percentage of women in the job as a whole will only reach 50 percent after a generation, when the last male hired before you started your scheme retires.

Most Canadian supporters of affirmative action don't want their targets reached this slowly. The Ontario College of Art recently set aside 100 percent of positions of a certain type for women. A proposal at a university department I know is to hire two-thirds women over the next fifteen years.

These schemes can't be justified on the ground of removing barriers or ensuring that the best candidates are hired. They clearly involve selecting people who are not, in the traditional sense, most qualified. An honest defence of them must recognize this and show why, despite it, the schemes are still justified.

There are two arguments that attempt this. They're discussed in the next essay.

QUESTIONS FOR DISCUSSION

1. Is any one of the three forms of affirmative action — tie breaking, extra points, and quotas — ethically more or less acceptable than the others?

2. Shouldn't we let businesspeople and managers make hiring decisions as they think best? Aren't they better judges of candidates' qualifications than affirmative action bureaucrats?

3. Why does the argument about removing "systemic barriers" not justify a scheme that will move a work force from 20 percent women to 50 percent women in ten years? (Assume that only 25 percent of the old work force will retire during this period.)

Affirmative Action:
More Radical Arguments

*A*ffirmative action means giving preference in hiring to selected groups, such as women. Its official Canadian justification is that this will ensure the best-qualified person is hired, that "systemic" barriers don't prevent talented women from advancing as they should.

This justification works for some affirmative action. If managers systematically undervalue women, forcing them to prefer women can improve their hiring decisions. But it doesn't justify all the affirmative action in Canada.

Many Canadian schemes involve hiring above a target percentage, say, above 50 percent women, so the target is reached in a particular work force in ten or twenty years. They clearly prefer people who are in the traditional sense less qualified, that is, who will do less well in the job on a day-to-day basis.

An honest justification of these schemes must recognize this. Is an honest justification possible?

One defence of the schemes points to the long-term consequences of affirmative action. It admits affirmative action has short-term costs in lost job efficiency but claims these are outweighed by long-term social benefits.

For some, the main benefit is just achieving, as quickly as possible, a representative work force, one where the proportion of women in top jobs equals their proportion in the population. This is morally dubious, however. Any morally significant benefits must be benefits to individuals, not groups.

But affirmative action does benefit individuals, by changing people's attitudes. If the belief that women are inferior persists in Canada, either consciously or subconsciously, it's partly because women aren't sufficiently prominent in Canadian life. Moving them quickly into important jobs can help dispel that belief and the many harms it does. Seeing female lawyers and managers can dispel sexist stereotypes.

Equally important are the changes in the attitudes of women. What you aspire to in life depends on what you think you can do, which depends in large part on what people like you have done before. Women in prominent jobs can be role models, encouraging young women to work for similar success. If the young women achieve success, this will benefit both them and society, which now wastes much of their potential.

If affirmative action has these long-term benefits, is it therefore justified? If consequences were all that mattered morally, the answer would be yes. But some moralists deny this, saying any policy is wrong that discriminates by race or gender. Affirmative action's end may be good, but it doesn't justify discriminatory means.

The issue is tricky, however. Imagine that there's a job for which intelligence is used as a qualification, so the more intelligent are hired ahead of the less intelligent. Can the less intelligent complain of discrimination? Is hiring by

IQ unjust? We want, I think, to say no — but on what basis? Why is IQ discrimination not wrong?

There seems to be just one possible argument: hiring by intelligence isn't wrong because intelligent candidates will do the job better. And that's important because society benefits when the job is done better.

This argument implies a more general one. Discrimination on any basis is wrong if its social consequences are bad, but not otherwise. Discrimination that does good is morally permitted.

Using this test, race and sex discrimination come out usually wrong. They hire less able candidates and, when the group discriminated against is disadvantaged, perpetuate harmful attitudes against it. But this isn't the case for discrimination in favour of the disadvantaged, as in affirmative action. This discrimination can have overall good consequences and therefore be justified.

This thinking appears in the Canadian Charter of Rights and Freedoms, whose equality clauses explicitly exempt programs aimed at "the amelioration of conditions of disadvantaged individuals or groups." If these programs do social good, they don't violate equality and aren't forbidden.

We've looked at a second justification of affirmative action: that even when it doesn't hire the most qualified person, it has good long-term consequences. A third argument says that affirmative action is required as compensation for past injustices. If women and Natives were discriminated against in the past, they should be compensated today in the form of preferential hiring.

Though common in U.S. discussions, this argument isn't heard as much in Canada. Despite this, the objections to it are often, irrelevantly, introduced into Canadian debate.

One objection is that affirmative action benefits only the least disadvantaged members of the selected groups, those doing well enough to apply for high-profile jobs. Another is that it places the entire burden of compensation on a few white males who are no more guilty of the injustice than anyone else. If they didn't cause the past discrimination, why should they, alone, make up for it?

I believe these objections can be answered. If the effects of injustice are widespread and long lasting, they can affect all members of a group, including those doing comparatively well. (If worse-off members of the group aren't benefited by affirmative action, they should get some other compensation.) And the white males, though not specially guilty of the past injustice, may be its prime beneficiaries, competing successfully against women and Natives who would beat them given an equal chance. Since they're the big winners from the injustice, it's only fair that they give up their ill-gotten gains.

In the United States, it would be vital to evaluate these claims about compensation. But in Canada the compensation argument merely supplements two more common justifications of affirmative action — about hiring the best people and promoting long-term social good. Honest people can disagree about how much affirmative action these justifications support, but, as our Charter recognizes, they do support some.

QUESTIONS FOR DISCUSSION

1. Would affirmative action have just the long-term good consequences suggested in the early part of the essay, or would there also be some bad consequences? If so, would the good or the bad consequences be greater?

2. How do we decide whether discrimination on some basis — by race, religion, intelligence, work experience, interview performance — is or is not wrong?

3. Is it unfair that the entire burden of affirmative action falls on those few white males who would have secured jobs or law school places without affirmative action but are passed over with it?

When Joining Golf Clubs, All Should Be on a Par

*H*all Thompson's loose lips cost ABC-TV a lot of money. The founder of the Shoal Creek Golf Club in Birmingham, Alabama, the site of the 1990 Professional Golfers Association Championship, told a reporter his club does not admit black members. In the ensuing uproar, several sponsors withdrew from ABC's tournament coverage, leaving a shortfall of over $2 million.

Shoal Creek's practice was not unusual. At the time of the controversy, a Philadelphia newspaper surveyed 34 of the leading golf clubs around that city and found that 33 had no black members. Of the 21 clubs scheduled to host major championships in the United States in the five years after 1990, 15 admitted no blacks and at least 1 admitted no women.

Nor is this practice illegal, either in the United States or in most provinces of Canada. Most provincial human rights laws forbid discrimination in the provision of goods and services "customarily available to the public." Under the current interpretation, the last phrase exempts private clubs. (The exception is Ontario, whose antidiscrimination law is not restricted to "public" services. But Ontario has a clause allowing recreational clubs to discriminate on the basis of sex.)

There are some areas where discrimination clearly must be illegal. It would be intolerable if the government, or landlords and companies operating in the public economy, withheld services on the ground of race or sex. Normal accommodation and jobs must be equally available to all.

But there are also areas where discrimination, however distasteful, must be allowed. If someone uses racial criteria in deciding whom to marry or ask to dinner, the law should not interfere in this private choice. The same goes for some choices about accommodation and jobs. Provincial human rights laws contain exemptions for people renting a room in their house, where a boarder will share their bathroom and kitchen, or hiring a private nurse to tend them at home. These too fall within a private sphere where discrimination is allowed.

Where does a members-only golf club fit on the scale from public to private? Is it more like a company offering services in the public economy, or a group of friends associating with people they find congenial?

The issue is complicated because there are different ways of defining privacy. One test looks at a club's admission procedures. If these procedures are rigorous, checking new members seriously for their social compatibility with old ones, the club is private. A second test looks at the club's functions or activities. Only if these are not commercial or business-related is the club private.

Those who think golf clubs shouldn't be allowed to discriminate use the second test. They note that a club isn't just a place to hit a little ball. It's where a city's elite congregate, where they make business contacts and deals. To be excluded from it is to be shut out from full participation in commercial life.

This argument is less compelling for a golf club than for a business club, such as the Petroleum Club in Calgary, which until recently excluded women. The golf club does have a largely sporting function. But many people join clubs, especially the exclusive ones, partly for the contacts they can make: membership offers more than golfing privileges. And the privacy argument is also weaker here. Sharing a fairway with someone you don't like is hardly as intimate as sharing your home.

When so much in business depends on whom you know, what looks private can in effect be public. Given this, the freedom of association that protects informal gatherings should not be extended to formal clubs, where mere admission can confer status. A law committed to equality should require these clubs to be open to all.

Of course, legality isn't the only issue: things the law should allow can be immoral and worth fighting by other means. (If someone won't dine with blacks, you shouldn't dine with him or her.) Stung by the Shoal Creek controversy, the PGA has decided to hold future tournaments only at clubs that accept minority memberships. Let's hope the moral and financial pressure this applies will do as much good as a formal legal ban.

QUESTIONS FOR DISCUSSION

1. Are there morally important differences between discrimination by government agencies, by large corporations, and by individuals in their private lives?

2. Can the owners of factories or large apartment buildings argue that since it's their property, they should be free to decide who works or lives there using whatever criteria they like, even racial criteria?

3. If a golf club screens prospective members carefully to check that their personality fits existing members but is also a place where important business contacts are made, is the club predominantly private or public?

Mandatory Retirement Is Discriminatory, but Not Unfair

*I*n 1990, the Supreme Court of Canada upheld the constitutionality of mandatory retirement at hospitals, universities, and community colleges. Some of these institutions, the court held, are not public and therefore not subject to the Charter of Rights. (The Charter protects citizens against governments, not against each other.) At those that are public, mandatory retirement does infringe the equality rights in the Charter but is justified under Section 1 as a "reasonable limit" in a democratic society.

The court's increasing use of Section 1 to uphold laws it agrees infringe rights is disturbing, but here it led to the right result. Mandatory retirement involves discrimination by age, but not unjust discrimination.

The central forms of discrimination — by race, sex, or religion — operate consistently through time: some people are always winners and some are always losers. If these kinds of discrimination are practised, some people are treated better and some worse throughout their lives.

If we view mandatory retirement just in the present, it too seems to involve differences in treatment: the old get no job opportunities and, as a result, the young get more opportunities. But this appearance vanishes if we look beyond the present. If mandatory retirement has been in place long enough, the people now being forced from their jobs had expanded opportunities when they were young. And the people filling their shoes will likewise be retired when they reach 65.

Unlike discrimination by race, sex, or religion, mandatory retirement treats everyone the same in their lives as a whole. Everyone has a better chance at a good job when they're young, and no chance when they're old.

In other contexts, we recognize that what matters isn't equal treatment at particular moments, but equal treatment through time. A young boy may complain that it's unfair that his sister has a birthday party today and he does not. Here we remind him that on another day of the year, he gets a party and she does not.

The argument is not that everyone benefits equally from mandatory retirement: there are net winners and net losers. The net winners are people with modest natural talents. They get better jobs than they otherwise would when young, so they benefit at the front end. And they don't lose later, since their employers wouldn't want them working past 65. (With "performance review," they might even be forced out before 65.) The net losers are people with the greatest talents. They don't gain when young since, given their talents, they'd get the best jobs anyway. And they do lose later, since their companies would want them on as long as possible.

But, as philosopher Gary Wedeking of the University of British Columbia has shown, the differing effects on these groups aren't age discrimination, since the groups aren't distinguished by age. Nor are they unjust discrimination. People with more talent already lead more favoured lives, with more interesting and highly paid jobs. To transfer some of their gains to those who are less fortunate is, on many views, not to diminish but to increase equity.

There are other arguments for and against mandatory retirement. Supporters call it a humane way to create job opportunities for the young. Instead of the trauma of performance review, with older workers evaluated to see when they can be forced out, there's an automatic rule for everyone.

Opponents say it's inefficient, replacing the best older workers with less talented youngsters, and also harms those older workers. When your job is your life, it can be terrible to lose it.

But these aren't arguments of justice, and they don't raise constitutional issues. The Charter of Rights isn't an all-purpose document for reviewing government actions. It leaves governments free to choose what they think are the best means to democratically selected goals, so long as the goals and policies don't violate individuals' rights. Mandatory retirement doesn't violate rights — its pros and cons are therefore for legislatures to assess.

QUESTIONS FOR DISCUSSION

1. Is age discrimination similar to discrimination by race, gender, or religion, or is it fundamentally different?

2. Why is it important to ask who gains and who loses from mandatory retirement in their lives as a whole?

3. How good an argument for mandatory retirement is it that, with it in place, companies will
   let workers stay in their jobs until 65 whom
   they would otherwise force out before 65 for
   fear that they would stay into their 70s?

Can You Fire Someone for Being Too Fat?

*J*esse Mercado, security guard, knows how tough it can be if you're fat. He was fired from his job at the *Los Angeles Times* even though there were no complaints about his performance. The reason? He was overweight.

In the United States, private companies normally pay for their employees' health insurance. Worried by rising insurance costs, some companies are now refusing to employ people they see as health risks, such as fat people and smokers.

This couldn't happen in Canada, given our universal medicare system. But a Canadian company might want to have the most productive work force possible. And it might believe that fat people on average have shorter careers, take more sick days, and are snoozier in the afternoon after eating larger lunches.

Granting for argument's sake that these beliefs are true, would a company be wrong to use them as a partial basis for hiring decisions? The National Association to Advance Fat Acceptance, a U.S. lobby group, would say yes. If we agree, we think we know why.

In using statistical facts about fat people to decide about a particular job applicant, the company isn't treating the applicant as an individual. It isn't looking at qualities he or she has, but at properties of a group he or she belongs to.

This simple explanation won't do. Unless we're extreme radicals, we think there are some legitimate bases for hiring decisions: aptitude, intelligence, job experience. But it's not as if *everyone* who is more intelligent or experienced will perform better than *anyone* who is less intelligent or experienced. There's again just a statistical relationship. To hire by brain power or years of work is, as with weight, to prefer members of a group that performs better only on average. Or consider school grades. It's not as if *every* A student will be better than *any* B student: the difference, again, is only between the groups.

There are some statistical facts that we don't allow in hiring decisions. Maybe in today's society blacks last a shorter time on the job than whites, or women applicants to medical school are less likely to end up practising as full-time doctors. You can't use these facts against blacks or women — that's race or gender discrimination.

As a society, we've decided that facts about some groups, such as the less intelligent, can be used in hiring decisions, but facts about other groups cannot. Where do facts about body weight belong? In the United States, there's a growing tendency to exclude these facts. Nineteen states have passed laws forbidding discrimination by "lifestyle." Jesse Mercado sued the *Los Angeles Times* and won $500 000 plus reinstatement in his job.

The trick is to justify this stand, or any division between allowed and forbidden statistical facts. Any true generalization will help a company hire, in the long run, better workers, which will benefit it and society. So why are some generalizations ruled out?

Maybe the answer is this: To be morally justified, discrimination against a group must benefit the members of that very group. It's not enough that it benefits society as a whole; the people it excludes must end up better off.

This test seems to be passed by discrimination against the less intelligent. They gain more than they lose when the most important jobs are done by those who can do them best. But race and gender discrimination fail the test. Even when they have overall good effects, they don't serve the long-term interests of blacks and women.

Discrimination by weight also fails the test. The small social gains that come from excluding Jesse Mercado from a job don't outweigh the losses to Jesse Mercado. Since he's on balance harmed, the policy is wrong.

We've partially recognized this in Canada. One effect of public medicare is to prevent discrimination by health status. The less fit pay no more for health care than the hale and robust. It's a logical extension of this to forbid weight discrimination in hiring. We've agreed, as a society, to bear the extra health costs of fat people. We should follow through by accepting the small inefficiencies that result from equality in hiring for the heavier set.

Claims for equality aren't unending; not every group has a right to non-discrimination. But fat people have a claim of the same kind as racial minorities and women.

QUESTIONS FOR DISCUSSION

1. If it is wrong to discriminate by "lifestyle," would it be wrong to fire a worker for being an alcoholic or for repeatedly getting injured playing dangerous sports on the weekend?

2. Imagine that a medical school knows that 95 percent of men who are admitted will practise medicine full-time after graduation but only 80 percent of women will, but cannot tell which individual men or women will make which choice. May the school give some preference in admissions to male over female applicants?

3. In Canada's medicare system, those who are ill or get injured, even recklessly, pay no more for their health care than those who never see a doctor. Is this fair?

Why Equality Doesn't Mean Treating Everyone the Same

*J*udy Rebick raised some hackles. Commenting on the Constitution, the president of the National Action Committee on the Status of Women said, "We understand that equality doesn't mean treating everyone the same way." There were angry letters to *The Globe and Mail* recalling George Orwell's *Animal Farm*, where "some animals are more equal than others."

Ms. Rebick's concept of equality isn't Orwellian — it's obviously correct. Think about people with disabilities. As a society, we spend more on these people than on those without disabilities. We build special access ramps to buildings; we subsidize wheelchairs; we provide closed-captioned TV news. If equality meant treating everyone the same way, this would all be unjust. There would be Charter challenges to handicapped parking zones: they reserve the best parking spots for a limited few. But we don't take this line. We recognize that treating people with disabilities the same way as others would be unjust: it would ignore their special needs.

Equality means giving everyone an equal chance to participate in social life: an equal chance to make choices, and to offer themselves for choice — as a friend or employee — by others. In an ideal world, equality could be secured by treating everyone the same, but when some face special obstacles, they need help to overcome them.

The idea isn't to produce "equality of results," where everyone has the same job or income. Some people, given an equal chance to participate in social life, may choose not to, preferring leisure and quiet to prestigious but high-pressure work. Others may lose in fair competition for this work, because they lack the talent for it. What equality demands is just the chance at fair competition.

The different treatment that equality requires for people with disabilities can also apply in hiring. Hence the appropriateness of some "employment equity."

A University of Calgary report notes that in 1990, only 22 percent of professors hired at the university were women, even though in 1988, 30.6 percent of Canadian Ph.D.s went to women. This may be an accident, based on the fields the hiring was in. (There are ten times more women Ph.D.s in English than in physics.) But often this kind of discrepancy reflects "systemic discrimination" — not conscious bias against women, but hidden factors that work against them.

People on hiring committees may have a mental picture of a good candidate, based on their experience of successful past employees. If these employees have mostly been male, the picture will be male. A qualified woman may fit it less well than a less qualified man.

Systemic discrimination creates a disability for those who face it—not a physical disability, but a socially imposed one. And it demands steps to remove it, such as a rule requiring that a woman be hired unless a man is "demonstrably better."

This argument doesn't justify everything done under the name "employment equity." The Calgary report recommends a goal for the university of 30 percent women professors by the year 2000. Given the expected rate of retirements, reaching this goal would require hiring roughly 40 percent women over the next decade—more than the current proportion of Ph.D.s. If this more ambitious goal is justified, it must be on other grounds.

Sometimes gender or race is a positive qualification for a job. A university is for education, but students don't learn only in lectures. They learn by interacting with each other, which is why some universities go for a socially diverse student body. Students also learn by interacting with their professors. A professoriate that is overwhelmingly male sends a skewed message about who can and cannot succeed; in these conditions, a woman, as a woman, can improve the university's teaching.

Or we can care about equality in the next generation: giving its young women the same encouragement and role models that young men have always had. This is another reason for preferring women professors

In *Animal Farm*, some animals are "more equal than others" because they want a better chance at the good things in life. This is wrong: equality demands an equal chance for all. But sometimes giving that equal chance means treating people differently—levelling a playing field that would otherwise be full of bumps and hollows.

QUESTIONS FOR DISCUSSION

1. What does society owe by way of "equal treatment" to those with physical disabilities, and why?

2. If society were to give everyone a truly equal chance to participate in social life, how much change would be required in education, the rights of families, inheritance law, and so on?

3. Does a university teach better, and serve society better, if it has a racially diverse group of professors and students?

Part Eight

Ethics of Personal Life

*E*thical issues arise not only in large-scale public policy choices, but also in our personal lives. How should we treat our friends? Is it wrong to gossip? May we lie to our children? The principles relevant to these issues are the same as those for public policy choices, but they must be applied in light of the fact that some people matter more to us than others. Our intimates are people we care about in special ways, and this affects how we ought to treat them.

Could You Love a Perfect Clone of Your Spouse?

*I*f you love your spouse, you love him or her partly for certain qualities: the smile, the ready wit, that plucky perseverance. At the very least, there are some people whose qualities mean you could never love them. You could never love someone who was wimpish and dull.

But this poses a problem. You know your spouse isn't unique in the world: there are other people with the same qualities, some to a higher degree. If one of those people came along, would you or should you love them more? It sounds like the worst kind of emotional promiscuity.

Maybe the question isn't realistic: you'll never meet someone with just your spouse's combination of qualities. But let your imagination roam. Your spouse has decided to leave you but doesn't want you to suffer. So he or she has a clone made who can stay with you afterward. Does this leave you no worse off? Or, better still, your spouse has, Star Trek–style, a perfect molecular duplicate made. It shares not only his or her looks and personality, but all your spouse's memories and understanding of you. If you want, some annoying little traits can be removed. Are you then better off for the breakup?

We want very much to say no, and we think we know why. True love, we say, isn't aimed just at a person's qualities, but at the person themselves. The philosophical question is what this means.

Some people have the following idea. Behind each person's qualities is the real person, the essential person, and what you love is that — not just the qualities, but the self that has them.

But this idea won't stand up. If the real self has no qualities, it must be like a globe of Lucite — hard, featureless, and transparent. And how can you love a globe of Lucite? More importantly, how can you love one globe of Lucite more than another, your spouse's more than Madonna's or Brian Mulroney's? If they have no qualities, all "real selves" must be indistinguishable.

The correct explanation is more banal but also more interesting. Among your spouse's qualities are some no one else could have: historical properties, concerning his or her past.

The two of you share a history. There was that weekend in Paris, the flu you nursed your spouse through, the children you both raised. If you love your spouse partly for having shared in this history, then you love him or her for something that can't be copied. No clone or duplicate could be the very person that did those things.

It's puzzling that we care so much about historical qualities. Why base our attachments on past events rather than on what people are like now? But we do it, and not just with people. As with a spouse, we can become attached to a particular car or sweater because of the things it has taken us through. Maybe we won't drive an old beater way past the point of cost-effectiveness, but we don't just junk it at the first rattle.

If historical qualities were all we cared about, our loves would be eternal, as romantics think they should be. ("Love is not love," Shakespeare says, "that alters when it alteration finds.") But this surely goes too far. Even if love is aimed partly at qualities that can't be lost or copied, it's aimed partly at properties that can. If enough changes in your spouse or you, then despite your history, your love may die.

If this happens, you may retain some fondness of your ex, just because of your history. You may wish him or her well from a distance, remembering what you shared.

Or your love may turn to anger or hatred. (It's ugly, but it happens.) Then your history will make a nasty feeling stronger. You'll resent your ex more than you would any clone or perfect copy.

The capacity for feelings directed at particular objects is one that distinguishes us from other animals. But it's a curious capacity, aimed partly at the past. We respond not just to what people are, but to what they have been. Is this a sensible response? Or would perfectly rational beings be able to love clones?

QUESTIONS FOR DISCUSSION

1. Should true love be eternal? If you would stop loving a person if he or she lost certain qualities, does that show that your love isn't the very best love?

2. Why should we care about people as individuals rather than just for their qualities? Why, in particular, should we care about their history, or the things they did with us?

3. Is there something morally unsettling about a person who falls in love with a second spouse almost immediately after his or her first spouse dies?

Gossip: Curtailing the Telling of Tales

*T*he two most popular activities in North America are probably daydreaming and gossip. But let's put aside daydreams: this essay is about gossip.

Gossip is talk about other people, but not all such talk is gossip. Consider a good obituary, which tries to make sense of someone's life as a whole and to identify its greatest achievements. It is paradigmatically not gossip.

Gossip deals with particular facts about others that are found interesting as particular facts: who they're kissing, who did or didn't like their lecture, why they aren't invited to the party.

There are two attitudes to gossip: some enjoy it unabashedly, the rest of us feel uneasy. We gossip (who doesn't?), but worry that doing so is distasteful. Why the unease?

First, we may worry, gossip is trivial. Fixed on personal details, it's not about modern poetry, the future of socialism, or anything intellectually important.

Second, gossip is often inaccurate, and predictably so. Since it's about people who aren't

present, it lacks the obvious check on truthful-
ness — the testimony of its subject. This is especially troubling when so much gossip is malicious,
aimed to denigrate or even hurt.

But even accurate gossip can be distasteful.
Often it prompts *Schadenfreude:* pleasure in another
person's pain. Someone has lost money or been
dressed down by the boss; when you hear about
it, you get a nasty pleasure out of thinking they're
worse off than you.

Most importantly, gossip, which occurs
behind someone's back, invades their privacy. It
prevents them from determining who knows or
discusses what about their personal lives. It takes
away their control of others' thoughts about
them.

These are the charges. But a more recent
trend is to embrace gossip as something positive,
as a source of moral and emotional knowledge.
Since gossip is traditionally associated with
women, this line is taken especially by some
feminists.

These feminists don't deny that gossip can be
trivial and malicious. But they insist that serious
gossip, the most valuable kind, is different.
Serious gossip starts from personal details — it
wouldn't be gossip if it didn't. But it moves on to
questions of motivation ("Why did she do that?"),
both about the individual and about people
generally. It passes over from storytelling to
psychology.

It also passes over to morality. Serious gossips
want to know whether the actions they're discussing were right or wrong, and they exchange
views about this until, perhaps, a consensus is
reached.

There is a theory of knowledge contained in
this view. It's not enough, feminists argue, to
know universal psychological laws or moral
principles. You have to know how to apply them

to particular cases, and that's what you learn in gossip.

This defence of gossip answers many of the objections, but not the one about privacy. If anything, it makes that objection worse. That people should discuss events in your life is one thing. That they should analyze your deep motivations — your "sense of inadequacy" or "fear of your father" — seems far more invasive.

McGill University philosopher Louise Collins addressed this objection in a paper given at the 1990 Canadian Philosophical Association meetings. Letting people themselves decide which aspects of their lives they'll be judged by, she argued, encourages hypocrisy and self-deception. By refusing to take people on their own terms, gossip opposes these vices.

This argument may justify some gossip. When people put out a specific image of themselves — as a Lothario or the boss's favourite — they make the subject public and so permit talk about it. They want us to accept the image on their authority, but we needn't do so. We can look for other, perhaps contrary, evidence and pass it on by gossip. But sometimes people don't put out any image.

A friend once suggested discussing the sex life of a married couple we knew. I said I'd never thought about the subject and wouldn't now; they'd prefer me not to. He said that what they didn't know couldn't hurt them, an argument I rejected. The couple hadn't broadcast any image of their sex life; they wanted us to have no view about it. There was no room for hypocrisy or deception, and gossip could only be invasive.

In some cases people clearly license gossip, in others clearly not. But there are grey areas. Does merely moving into a neighbourhood license gossipy speculation about you? If a new couple hold hands in a public place, is it all right to pass on the news?

These are tough cases, but the general point is clear. When people license gossip about themselves, we can take the opportunity for entertainment and enlightenment. When they don't, we should feel more than uneasy.

QUESTIONS FOR DISCUSSION

1. Could gossip be ethically all right just because it's fun?

2. Does gossip really "invade" people's privacy? Must they really "license" us to talk about them?

3. Is it morally worse, or is it less bad, to gossip about close friends than about mere acquaintances?

Friendship: A Mixture of Love and Respect

$\mathcal{E}$nglish has no good word for the person you aren't married to but live with as if you were. "Partner" and "significant other" are too bland; "lover" invites the question, "How well does he or she do it?"

There's another bit of language missing. We have no word for what's common to our relationships with friends on the one hand and spouses or lovers on the other. These relationships differ, especially in the intensity of feeling they involve. But they're also similar, and we have no word that expresses how.

Fortunately, thought can go where language doesn't, and we can ask, "What is a friend?" (taking the milder word for the whole category). What defines our relationship to all those people who are special to us?

One theory says our friends (including spouses) are people we love, or love more than we love others. But this theory is inadequate: if all you have is love, you haven't got enough.

What is love? If you love a person, you prefer his or her company to other people's. And you care about them, wanting them to be happy. To some extent you want happiness for any human being, but if you love a particular person you care especially about his or her happiness.

Usually, this caring involves a kind of egoism. You want not just that your loved one be happy, but that *you* be an important source of their happiness. This is most obvious in sexual love: you want your lover to have sexual pleasure, but you're hardly indifferent about where he or she gets it.

This is sometimes denied in sentimental fiction. In Charles Dickens's *A Tale of Two Cities*, Sydney Carton, who loves the heroine Lucie, takes the place on the guillotine of the man she loves, to ensure her future happiness. ("It is a far, far better thing, etc.") But this isn't human. In Carton's place, most of us would want not just that Lucie live happily, but that she live happily *with us*, being made happy by our actions.

Especially when it involves this egoism, love is a force of attraction, bringing two people closer. They come together to take pleasure in each other's company and to give pleasure in return.

Reflecting this, some writers portray complete friendship as a merging or union of two natures in one. But these images are inadequate. At its fullest, friendship involves not just love but respect, where respect is an opposite force of repulsion.

Imagine that you come upon your friend's diary. If you love him or her, you'll be more curious about its contents than you would be about a stranger's diary. You want to know your friend, to understand his or her deepest thoughts, and here's a chance to do so.

But you will or should also be more hesitant to open this diary. Invading someone's privacy —

taking away from them the power to decide who knows what about their inner life — will be especially distasteful if they're a friend. Counterbalancing your love here is greater respect, or a greater reluctance to interfere with someone's freedom. It often conflicts with attraction.

Imagine that your friend has a job offer that would take him or her to another city. You may have reasons of love for hoping they don't accept it: you don't want to be separated from them, you think they'll be unhappy away from you. Respect insists that you leave them free to decide the issue themselves. You may try to persuade them against the move but mustn't go beyond that to pressuring.

In these examples, respect is given to something your friend shares with other people: free choice. But there's also respect directed at him or her as an individual.

We have self-esteem, philosophers say, when we think our goals in life are valuable and we are confident we can achieve them. Esteem can also be given to a friend: you can be confident about his or her achieving valuable goals. When it is given, it is a further check on attraction.

Imagine that your friend's job offer is important for advancement in their career and the full development of their potential. Then you have another reason for non-interference. If you didn't value their potential you might be happiest if they stayed with you. But if you esteem their life goals, you must sometimes stand back and let your friend pursue them.

These ideas about friendship come from the German philosopher Immanuel Kant. He said our friends are people we both love and respect more than others, where love is a force of attraction and respect keeps us apart. Kant's picture is more complicated than one where friendship involves only love and only a blending of natures. If love and respect conflict, we must balance them against each other, and won't always do so to each other's satisfaction.

But Kant's picture is more satisfying. If women today reject traditional marriages, it's partly because these marriages didn't involve both of Kant's elements. A traditional husband loved his wife: he wanted her company and cared about her happiness. But he didn't include her in important decisions ("Honey, we've been transferred to Winnipeg") and he didn't seriously value her abilities. She might be a good homemaker and mother, but in his eyes these weren't things that really mattered.

We can enjoy our time with friends and revel in our mutual love. But let's resolve, with Kant, not to let our love swamp our mutual respect.

QUESTIONS FOR DISCUSSION

1. Is it accurate to describe love as a force of attraction and respect as a force of repulsion?

2. Is it accurate to characterize friendship as involving the same feelings we have or should have toward all people, but to a higher degree? Or are some feelings unique to friendship?

3. If friendship involves not just love, but love and respect, is a mutually satisfying friendship easier or harder to maintain?

Why There Are Some Things Money Shouldn't Buy

*W*e're often told what money can't buy: love, happiness, respect. But there are also things we think it shouldn't buy, or that social norms say it's wrong to try to buy. Here are two examples from Jon Elster's *Nuts and Bolts for the Social Sciences* (Cambridge University Press).

If you arrive at a movie theatre after the show is sold out, you don't walk up to someone in line and offer to buy their place; if you do, you'll get disapproving looks. This kind of thing isn't done.

But why? Your offer won't harm anyone else in line, since they'll still get in. Nor will it harm the person you talk to. They can always say no, and if they don't it'll be because they prefer taking your money and seeing the film another night. The exchange will happen only if both you and they benefit—yet social norms say it shouldn't happen.

In another example, you pay your neighbour's son $10 to cut your grass, but you wouldn't pay

more: if he asked for $11, you'd do the job your-
self. This seems to show that you'd rather have
$11 than avoid cutting a lawn. But if your neigh-
bours offered you $20 to cut their grass, you'd
refuse angrily: again, this kind of offer isn't made.
Given your preferences, shouldn't you welcome it?

In these examples, bargains that economists
would say benefit both parties are forbidden by
social norms. (Call it a triumph of sociology over
economics.) The puzzle is why.

Maybe we think buying a movie place or a
neighbour's labour flaunts your wealth and power,
which can lead to envy and conflict. But this
needn't be so. You need be no richer than the
people in the movie line, just keener to see this
show tonight. And, as Professor Elster points out,
we don't mind other forms of flaunting. There's no
rule against wearing furs and diamonds in public.

I think we recognize that market relationships
are morally incomplete, and want something better in our private lives. But the point must be
stated carefully.

C.B. Macpherson, the late Canadian political
philosopher, said that free-market or capitalist
economies are built on "possessive individualism,"
an egoistic concern for just one's own welfare and
property. This is exaggerated. Market bargainers
respect each other's freedom, since they don't
coerce each other. And they deal with others only
in ways the others think will make them better off.

But this departure from egoism doesn't go very
far. In the market there's no call to improve others'
bargaining position; there's no worry if after a deal
they're still far worse off than you; and there's no
obligation to help them except in ways that also
help yourself.

In bargaining, your direct concern is just your
own welfare. You know that others are freely
protecting their welfare, and you may be glad
they are doing so. But within this constraint, you
go for the best deal or price for yourself.

However fine this is in public life, it's not something we would accept in a family. We wouldn't be pleased with a spouse or parent who left our interests for us to protect. We want some direct concern for our welfare and a readiness to sacrifice for it.

So it is, I think, in a neighbourhood. If your neighbours hired you to cut their lawn, you'd have to settle on a price. And the weighing of costs involved in bargaining would call forth a self-concern that's at war with the caring you want in your personal life.

It's the same, if more loosely, at the theatre. People in the movie line may be strangers, but this is entertainment, not business, and we don't want our evening spoiled by a contest of self-interests.

We humans aren't entirely selfish or entirely concerned for others, and how we mix the two varies between contexts. In economic life, we constrain our egoism just a little, by respect for each other's freedom. But in private life we think there are some things you shouldn't try to buy.

QUESTIONS FOR DISCUSSION

1. If both parties would gain from a contract, for example, to sell a place in a movie line, how can the contract be morally questionable?

2. Is a close friend a person you would especially want, or especially not want, to sell a car to?

3. Don't even our closest friendships rest implicitly on a bargain: you'll love and help your friend so long as he or she loves and helps you?

Do Children Have Rights?

*O*ne aim of the 1990 World Summit for Children, co-chaired by then Prime Minister Brian Mulroney, was to urge ratification of the United Nations Convention on the Rights of the Child. Now, children have rights, but they're not the same as the rights of adults.

Competent adults have a right of autonomy, a right to make free choices about their lives even if those choices aren't always best for them. They can choose a career that isn't best suited to their talents, or marry unwisely. It's their life, and so long as they don't harm others they're entitled to decide freely how it's lived.

Moralists disagree about how strong this right is. Some think it's absolute, so it's always wrong to interfere with a person's private choices. Others think the right can sometimes be outweighed. If a person's actions will be very harmful to himself or herself, others have a right and even a duty to intervene.

But however strong an adult's right to autonomy, it's not shared by children. A 10-year-old girl can't decide to stop going to school just because she doesn't like it. Nor does she even have the right to decide what time she goes to bed. It wouldn't do her serious harm to watch an extra half hour of TV, but it's not for her to make the choice.

This doesn't mean that parents should always boss around their kids. Sometimes they should let them make choices, so they can grow up knowing responsibility. But this isn't a matter of the children's rights. It concerns their long-term good, which is still in their parents' care.

So what are children's rights? A child can feel pain just like an adult, so if torture violates an adult's right it does the same to a child. Children also have a right to autonomy: the autonomy they will exercise in the future. They have what philosopher Joel Feinberg calls the "right to an open future," the right to enter adulthood with a great many options open to them and a developed capacity to choose among them.

Articles 28 and 29 of the U.N. convention affirm the child's right to education, which must be provided free of charge. Education increases a child's future earning power and imparts intrinsically valuable knowledge, but a further important function is to prepare him or her for a life of autonomous self-direction.

Education does this partly by increasing a child's options. Even if he or she later doesn't take the highest-paying job, it's important to have had it to choose against. Education also gives the child the intellectual tools needed to evaluate options rationally and make, in the fullest sense, a choice among them. And finally, education increases a child's awareness of possibilities. Through literature and the study of other cultures, children learn that there are other value systems and ways of living than those they're familiar with.

This right also imposes obligations on parents, who must likewise let their child grow up to choose freely. They act wrongly if they shield the child from exposure to beliefs and values other than their own, or pressure him or her unduly into becoming, say, a lawyer.

There's some balancing needed here, for parents, too, have rights: to base a family life on their values and to try to pass them on to their children. Perhaps the right balance is this: Parents needn't give equal time to all value systems but must at least let their child be exposed to lifestyles other than their own. They must leave options open, even if they don't encourage them all equally.

Some parents do more. A friend of mine, himself agnostic about religion, takes his children to church, because he wants them to grow up knowing enough about religion to make an informed choice about it. This is more than can be demanded as a child's right; parents who don't do it aren't wrong. But it respects the same future freedom that, at a lower level, is protected by right.

Children aren't now entitled to make choices that are bad for them, but they will be later on. This gives them an important right now: to be allowed to grow into adults who can make autonomous decisions about themselves.

QUESTIONS FOR DISCUSSION

1. If a parent thinks it's in a child's long-term interest to get used to making choices, why isn't the parent treating the child as having rights?

2. Is it morally acceptable for parents who believe in a fundamentalist religion to shield their child from influences, such as education in a public school, that may undermine the child's belief in that religion?

3. Are parents respecting a child's right to an "open future" if they express preferences about the career they want the child to pursue, or if they plan the child's education to prepare for that career?

Is It Wrong to Lie about Santa Claus?

I don't have kids, but I used to be one, and like all kids I was lied to. I was lied to about the Tooth Fairy; I was lied to about the Easter Bunny; and I was lied to about Santa Claus. I was told Santa exists when, in fact, he doesn't.

My parents tried to bring me up properly. They gave me a moral education, including the lesson that lying is wrong. But every Christmas they told me tales about reindeer and sleighs.

I don't resent this; I recall with pleasure the excitement it gave my early Christmases. And I don't think parents in general are wrong to tell their kids tales about Santa. The problem is to explain why.

We might try saying that talk of Santa isn't really a lie. Kids have tremendous powers of imagination, and what parents do at Christmas is just play along. But this won't do. The impetus for belief in Santa doesn't come from kids, it comes from parents. A tag on a present saying "To Geoffrey from Santa" makes a statement about where the present comes from. The statement isn't true; it's made to create a false belief; and that makes it a lie.

Or we might talk about the "deeper truth" in myths, the more profound lessons Santa can teach. But this is a cheat, for two reasons. It fudges the fact that, on the mundane issue of where presents come from, parents know what they're saying is false. (Real myth makers believe their myths.) And it finds a deeper truth where there doesn't seem to be one. In the Santa story, presents come from a stranger who gives gifts to everyone. In reality, presents come from parents who love their kids as individuals and give gifts to express this love. Isn't the reality more worth knowing than the myth?

What about Santa as moral educator, rewarding good kids but not bad ones? The fact is, it doesn't happen: all kids get presents. And the image of Santa, all jolly and ho-ho-ho, is inconsistent with a role as moral judge.

I think we have to admit that talk of Santa is a lie and can sometimes do harm. Some kids are bitterly disappointed when their illusion is shattered, and some are morally confused. ("Mom and Dad say not to lie, then do it themselves.") Fortunately, this doesn't happen often. Usually the Santa lie, befitting Christmas, is a white one.

For starters, the lie is only temporary. You tell kids about Santa now, but you'll straighten them out later. The deception isn't forever.

And the deception is a mild one. You don't take a falsehood and call it truth; you take a fiction and call it truth — a smaller distortion. This means the loss of the illusion is gentler. When kids are older they don't lose Santa entirely, they just think of him in a different way.

Finally, the deception is good for kids. Believing in Santa adds magic and excitement to Christmas; the anticipation is keener, the delight sharper. Parental love is fine and even profound, but a guy from the North Pole is far more exotic.

These reasons wouldn't justify lying to an adult. Adults have a right not to be lied to, even if the lie would benefit them. Maybe there are distressing facts about what their spouse is up to or how their father made his money. It would hurt them to know, but they've a right not to be deceived.

Kids don't have this right. (They have some rights of adults, but not all.) Parents needn't tell them hurtful facts, and if kids ask awkward questions, parents can lie. ("Did Mom and Dad fight last night? It was a little disagreement, all patched up now.") A parent's main duty is to do what's good for kids, and giving them fun is part of that duty.

This isn't a profound or spiritual argument. The main reason why lies about Santa are white is that they make Christmas fun. And this reason could one day be outweighed by contrary reasons. If more kids got morally confused — if more stopped thinking they shouldn't lie — we'd have to change our ways. For now, fortunately, this isn't necessary.

So yes, Virginia, you can tell your kids there's a Santa Claus. The story didn't hurt you, and it probably won't hurt them.

QUESTIONS FOR DISCUSSION

1. Why don't children have a general right not to be lied to?

2. The figure of Santa Claus comes from the Christian story of St. Nicholas. Does it therefore express an important religious or moral truth?

3. Does Christmas as it is celebrated today —
   with both carols and commercialism — teach
   children good or bad lessons about life?

Part Nine

Violence and War

*P*acifists believe that any use of force is morally wrong, but most of us disagree. We believe that although most violence is wrong, there are exceptions: self-defence, fighting in a just war, some forms of punishment. The essays that follow try to identify these exceptions, explaining in greater detail when the use of violence is morally permitted. The central essay is the one on self-defence. The conditions this essay lays down for legitimate self-defence turn out also to play a key role in the discussions of the just war and of capital punishment.

Going Too Far in Self-Defence

*I*n October 1990, nineteen Palestinians were killed on the Temple Mount in Jerusalem when Israeli police opened fire on a crowd that was throwing rocks at Jews gathered at the Wailing Wall below. The United Nations Security Council condemned the killings and called for a U.N. investigation of the incident.

The Israeli government rejected this call as hypocritical: the United Nations was ignoring the killings of sixteen Israelis in two attacks in Egypt and said nothing about the stone throwing that prompted its policemen's response.

It is certainly wrong when Israelis are murdered or crowds throw rocks. But sometimes both an action and the reaction to it are improper. And it's especially troubling when rights are violated by a government, which is supposed to protect them. Although it's bad when private citizens assault or kill each other, it's worse when the state does the same. It violates a special duty the state has to treat all citizens justly.

The charge against the Israeli police is of using excessive force. The police were protecting Jewish citizens, which it was proper for them to do. But there are proportionality rules governing the defence of rights and limiting the amount of force it morally allows.

A first rule says this force must not be too much greater than the force one is defending against. Imagine that someone is trying to tickle you against your will and the only way you can stop them is by shooting them dead. Here most of us think you have to let yourself be tickled. The forced tickling is wrong; but killing to prevent it would be going too far.

Specifying the exact content of this rule is difficult. Most of us think it can be right to kill to save your life. But what about to stop yourself from being raped or beaten up, or having your home broken into? Here reasonable people can disagree. There's an upper limit, but it's not clear exactly where it comes.

Some people use this *upper limit* rule to criticize the Israeli policemen's action on the Temple Mount. Killing to stop stone throwing, they say, is out of proportion. (This is a general criticism of the Israeli response to the Palestinian uprising or intifada: it counters mere stones with automatic weapons.) The criticism assumes, controversially, that killing is justified only to prevent something as serious as killing, and that the stone throwers did not threaten the lives of the Jews below.

But there's a second proportionality rule. Imagine that someone is coming at you with the intent to kill. You can stop them by killing them, but you can protect yourself just as well by shooting them with a tranquillizer gun, by wrestling them to the ground, or by just running away. Here, even though your life is at stake, it would be wrong for you to kill. You mustn't use more force than the minimum necessary to protect your rights, which in this case may be no force at all.

This *minimum necessary* rule has a corollary. If you've already successfully protected your rights but continue to use force against your attacker — keep beating or killing them — you use more than you need to defend yourself. Yet there's evidence that this is what the Israeli police did on the Temple Mount.

According to a *New York Times* report, the police kept shooting long after the Jews below had fled out of range of any rocks, and after the police themselves were in serious danger. There are bullet holes from automatic weapons on the inside walls of several mosques: not places from which you'd expect a serious threat. It seems that the police, having successfully controlled a dangerous crowd, went on gunning down its members. What started as a legitimate defence of rights, turned later into an attack.

Whether this in fact happened is not firmly settled; there are still conflicting reports. But that's why all parties should have welcomed a U.N. investigation. If the police didn't use excessive force, an impartial investigation would be the best way to establish this. If they did, the Israeli government would surely want to condemn their action. The reason isn't that Israel is held to higher moral standards than other nations. It's that it's always appalling when a state, whose job is to protect rights, turns away from that function and instead attacks them.

QUESTIONS FOR DISCUSSION

1. State the "upper limit" and "minimum necessary" rules carefully, and show how they differ from each other: describe a case where the first rule is satisfied but not the second, then

one where the second rule is satisfied but not the first.

2. Would it be wrong to kill someone if that was the only way to stop them from raping you, beating you up, breaking into your home, or stealing your car?

3. Why should attackers have any rights at all against defenders? If the attacker has committed aggression, why may the defender not do anything he or she likes in self-defence?

Morality and War: Cause and Intent

*P*acifists think war is always morally wrong. Those called "realists" think war is never wrong: it's beyond the scope of moral judgement. But the more common view is that war is sometimes right and sometimes wrong. The Second World War as fought by the Allies was morally right; if anything, not resisting Hitler would have been wrong. But other wars, such as maybe the Vietnam War, were wrong. And it would certainly be wrong if, say, the United States launched a nuclear strike against Canada just for fun.

What's called *just war theory* lays down conditions that a war must satisfy to be morally justified. We can explore this theory by applying it to the most widely publicized recent war, the U.S.-led Persian Gulf War against Iraq in 1991.

The first part of just war theory, called *ius ad bellum*, concerns when it's right for a nation to engage in war, or take up military force. Its first condition says the nation must have a *just cause*, or a good reason for war. In all versions of the theory, one just cause, and in some versions the only just cause, is to resist aggression. If your nation has been attacked by another, you can use force to stop the attack. If a third nation has been attacked, you can come to its defence. But a central primary just cause for war is resisting the unjust use of force by an aggressor nation.

Most commentators think the United States and its allies had a just cause in the Gulf War, namely responding to the aggression of Iraq, which had invaded and occupied its neighbour Kuwait in 1990. This wouldn't be a just cause if Iraq had a good reason for attacking Kuwait, but it didn't. Iraq had disputes with Kuwait: about some territory, about a Kuwaiti loan to Iraq, and about oil prices. But these were all reasons for negotiations, not war. In resorting to war Iraq acted unjustly, and gave its opponents a just cause to fight it.

Alongside the primary cause of resisting aggression, the allies had secondary just causes: to disarm Iraq so it wouldn't be able to try aggression again, and to deter it and other would-be aggressors by showing that aggression doesn't pay. These secondary causes can't on their own justify war. You can't attack another nation to disarm it if it hasn't yet aggressed. But if it has aggressed, you can have as another legitimate aim in war to disarm it. That's why the allies didn't have to stop the war immediately after expelling Iraq from Kuwait. They could keep fighting to disarm the Iraqi military, and in particular to destroy its chemical and nuclear weapons. The secondary causes are also important for other parts of just war theory, such as the proportionality and last resort conditions discussed in the next essay.

A second *ad bellum* condition says the war must be fought with a *right intention*. A nation must be motivated by the just cause and not by some selfish aim, such as its own self-aggrandizement. Many critics say the United States violated this condition in the Gulf War. Its leaders weren't motivated by concern for aggression, which they'd allowed in many other cases. They were fighting to maintain low oil prices for Americans or, worse, to boost their own popularity with American voters.

I think these criticisms can be answered, in either of two ways. One questions whether the right intention condition really belongs in just war theory. Don't we normally have the concept of "doing the right thing for the wrong reason"? And doesn't that imply that judgements about what is right are independent of judgements about motives? On this view, if the United States was motivated only by a concern for oil prices, it wasn't motivated in a very noble or admirable way. But in this case its ignoble motive, fortunately, led it to fight a war that was, independently, right.

The second answer says that if the right intention condition is understood properly, the United States did or at least could have satisfied it. Just war theory doesn't say a nation has to fight all the wars for which it has a just cause. If it does fight it does something permitted, but it also does something permitted if it decides not to get involved, as an officially neutral nation such as Switzerland never gets involved. But if a nation can fight no wars for which it has a just cause, it can surely fight some and not others. And it can surely decide which of these wars to fight on its own, perhaps partly selfish, grounds. Compare a body-guard who is morally permitted to come to the defence of anyone who is attacked, but who only in fact defends the person who pays his salary.

So imagine that the U.S.'s motivation was this: It would not fight a war unless it had a just cause such as resisting aggression, but it would also not fight unless its own interests were somehow at stake. (After the Gulf War, the United States announced a general military policy with exactly these two components.) Then its having a just cause would not be a sufficient condition for its fighting a war, since it would need a selfish motive as well. But a just cause would be a necessary condition, since it wouldn't fight without one. In this case I think the United States would satisfy any reasonable right intention condition, since it would be a necessary part of its motivation that it have a just cause. It's arguable that the United States had just this motivation in the Gulf War, and it's certain that its allies did.

So there's no good criticism of the Gulf War based on either the just cause or the right intention condition. But the *ad bellum* part of just war theory contains two other conditions about the effects of war. They're the subject of the next essay.

QUESTIONS FOR DISCUSSION

1. Does it make sense to evaluate wars as right and wrong, or is war somehow outside the scope of moral evaluation? Does the beginning of war mean that ordinary moral rules are suspended?

2. Is resisting aggression the only legitimate just cause for war? (This is the view taken by the United Nations.) If there are other just causes, what are they?

3. Is it true that the motives of a nation fighting a war are irrelevant to a judgement about the war's justice or rightness? Can a nation do the right thing for a wrong reason, or does its having a wrong reason make its action wrong?

Morality and War: Effects

$\mathcal{T}$o be morally justified, a nation resorting to war must have a just cause and (perhaps) a right intention. But there are two other conditions that just war theory says must be satisfied. War causes death and destruction, sometimes on a massive scale. A nation contemplating war must think in two ways about these effects.

A third, or *proportionality*, condition says that a war with a just cause is morally right only if the damage it will cause is not out of proportion to, or more serious than, the just cause. If achieving that cause will inevitably do more harm than good, the cause is not worth pursuing and the war is morally wrong.

Some people use this proportionality condition to argue that any nuclear war would be wrong. Whatever the cause at stake, they say, it could not justify risking the destruction of the planet. The condition is also important if there are just causes less serious than resisting aggression. Some people think a nation can have a cause for war if another nation interferes with its economic activity or harms some of its citizens. (One of the U.S.'s justifications for invading the Caribbean island of Grenada in the 1980s was an alleged threat to some American medical students there.) But it would obviously be wrong to start a massively destructive war to protect a small amount of trade or a few individuals.

The condition is harder to apply, though, to non-nuclear wars of resistance to aggression. Many people think defending the territorial integrity of nations is a very important cause, and justifies considerable military force. Despite this, some critics of the Persian Gulf War argued that it violated the proportionality condition.

One argument was that Kuwait was too small, distant, and undemocratic to be worth defending. This is a bad argument. A nation's size doesn't matter to the importance of its territorial integrity; if it did, large nations could invade small ones knowing it would be wrong for anyone to resist. Democracy does matter, but it was clear that the Kuwaitis vastly preferred their own government to occupation by Iraq. Their government was not ideal, but it was better than the alternative.

Two more serious arguments were that the war could cause massive environmental damage and that it could expand into something much larger. If Iraq drew Israel into the war against it, that could lead Arab nations opposed to Israel to join Iraq, causing a huge Middle Eastern conflagration. But neither of these things happened. There was environmental damage, but less than expected. And despite Iraq's bombing of it, Israel stayed out of the war. In fact, the co-operation among the allies against Iraq helped set the stage for a peace agreement between Israel and the Palestine Liberation Organization, and a partial settlement of their long-standing conflict.

In addition, an application of the proportionality condition must consider not only the primary just cause of resisting Iraqi aggression but also the secondary causes of disarming Iraq and deterring future aggression. What would the situation have been had the Gulf War not been fought? Iraq would have been in possession of Kuwait, militarily stronger, and poised to attack other neighbours. And a message would have been sent to other nations that even wanton aggression would not be opposed. When we count these effects, it's hard not to see the Gulf War as satisfying proportionality.

A fourth condition, the *last resort* or *necessity* condition, says war may only be used as a last resort. If there is some other way of achieving the just cause that will be less damaging, that way must be tried first, and opting immediately for war is wrong.

Again, many critics of the Gulf War said it violated this condition. In particular, they said it was wrong for the United States and its allies to start the war as quickly as they did rather than allowing more time for a negotiated settlement. After the Iraqi invasion of Kuwait, the United Nations imposed economic sanctions on Iraq, to induce a voluntary withdrawal. Those sanctions should have been given more time to work.

There are two problems with this argument. First, the last resort condition applies most naturally to just causes less serious than resisting aggression. If a nation's grievance is economic, then obviously it must try to address that grievance peacefully before resorting to war. But how does the condition apply to aggression? If Kuwait had resisted militarily when Iraq invaded in August 1990, surely that would have been morally acceptable. Likewise if the United States had come to its aid in August 1990. So why was the last resort condition not satisfied as of August 1990 and at any time thereafter? Surely we don't want to say that a nation must allow itself to be invaded and occupied so long as it thinks it will be able to persuade the occupier to leave after a couple of years.

Second, war only fails to be a last resort if there is some alternative that will achieve its just causes. In the case of the Gulf War, these causes included the secondary ones of deterring future aggression by Iraq and other nations. This required that any negotiated settlement not leave Iraq better off than before it invaded Kuwait; otherwise the message would be that you can commit aggression and win. But there was no evidence that a settlement meeting this condition would be accepted by Iraq. Before the war, diplomats from the Soviet Union and France contacted Iraq proposing deals with various benefits for Iraq. The United States condemned these proposals, saying there could be "no rewards for aggression," but Iraq rejected them all. And if it rejected deals that were unacceptably generous, why believe that it would accept a deal that was not?

There is, therefore, no reason to believe that the Persian Gulf War violated the last resort condition, or indeed any of the *ad bellum* conditions determining when the resort to war is justified. The war had a just cause; either it was fought with a right intention, or right intention does not matter; it was proportionate; and there was no less damaging way of achieving its aims. But there is another part of just war theory, concerned with how one fights a war once it has begun. Here our judgement of the Gulf War may be very different.

QUESTIONS FOR DISCUSSION

1. Can a war satisfy the proportionality condition but not the last resort condition and vice versa? If so, describe how this can happen.

2. What kind of destruction would be too much to justify resisting aggression against a country like Kuwait? What kind of destruction would not be too much? Is it possible to draw a line, even a rough one, here?

3. How long must nations try to resolve difficulties by negotiations before resorting to war?

Morality and War: How to Fight

*T*he first part of just war theory, *ius ad bellum*, lays down conditions that must be met before a nation's resorting to war is morally right. A second part, called *ius in bello*, concerns how the war is fought. It contains rules that the conduct of the war must follow for the war as a whole to be right.

Some of these rules forbid chemical weapons, certain deceptive stratagems, and the killing of prisoners. But the most important concern the treatment of non-combatants. These are people who aren't in the military and aren't directly helping it, as workers in weapons factories do. They're mostly ordinary civilians at home. There are two connected rules about non-combatants, called *discrimination* and *in bello proportionality*.

The discrimination rule says you mustn't direct military force at non-combatants; your targets must always be the enemy's military. The assumption is that a just war is fought against an army, not a people. In a war with a just cause you're responding to a threat, and that threat doesn't come from ordinary people at home.

This rule was massively violated in the Second World War: by Germany in its bombings of British cities, by Britain in its retaliatory bombings of German cities such as Dresden, and by the United States when it dropped atomic bombs on Hiroshima and Nagasaki. All these bombings were intended to demoralize the enemy by killing its civilians.

Some versions of just war theory say this kind of bombing is never right, because the discrimination rule is absolute. Others say the rule can be broken in very exceptional circumstances. In his book *Just and Unjust Wars*, American philosopher Michael Walzer argues that Britain's bombing of German cities early in the Second World War was justified, because then Germany was winning and there was no other way to resist a morally awful threat. But he thinks the later bombings, including of Dresden, were wrong, because by that time the tide of the war had turned. He also thinks the bombings of Hiroshima and Nagasaki were wrong, because they weren't needed to win the war. They meant winning didn't require an invasion of Japan, and so saved many soldiers' lives. But that doesn't justify directly killing civilians.

Even in its absolute form, the discrimination rule doesn't forbid all actions you know will harm non-combatants. It forbids only intending that harm as your end or as a means to your end. If you foresee that an action will kill civilians but don't intend this, then as far as discrimination goes the action is permitted.

This distinction between intending and foreseeing looks subtle but it's one we can draw in everyday life. If you go driving on a summer's night, you may know that you'll kill some mosquitoes. But you don't intend this as your end — you're not driving in order to kill mosquitoes — or as a means — you're not reaching your destination by killing mosquitoes. The distinction is also thought morally important in other areas. Current medical ethics doesn't allow active euthanasia, where a doctor kills a patient, even with his consent, to spare him pain. But medical ethics does allow giving a patient a pain-killing drug in the knowledge that one of its side effects will be to hasten the patient's death. The reason is that in the second case you foresee but don't intend the patient's death.

To see how the distinction works in the military context, imagine that a weapons factory is located in a neighbourhood where many civilians live. You may know that if you bomb the factory you will inevitably kill some civilians, because some bombs will miss their intended target. If you kill them only as a side effect of aiming at the factory, your action need not be wrong.

This doesn't mean that any action merely foreseeing harm to non-combatants is allowed; this is where the second rule, proportionality, comes in. It says that even actions that don't target non-combatants, and therefore satisfy discrimination, are morally wrong if the harm they cause non-combatants is out of proportion to, or more serious than, the good they will do in advancing the just cause. Imagine that the factory in the example above is very important to the other side, and that bombing it will kill only two or three civilians. Then the bombing is allowed. But if the factory is minor and the attack will kill thousands, the attack is forbidden. Given the special status of non-combatants, that much harm to them outweighs the small military gain.

Much criticism of the conduct of the Gulf War appealed to these two rules, but it's a little unclear which one fits best. The United States claimed that its bombing of Iraq was restricted to military targets and that its technologically advanced, "smart" weapons kept "collateral damage," or damage to civilians, to a minimum. The last claim was false; though only smart bombs made it onto TV, the vast majority of bombs used in Iraq were stupid. And the first claim was also questionable.

Though the United States kept itself to what it called military targets, its list of such targets was very long. It included not only army barracks and weapons factories but also electric power grids, water purification plants, and every bridge in the Iraqi capital of Baghdad. One could argue that by aiming at these, the United States was in effect targeting civilians and so violating discrimination. But even if one does not say this, the United States massively violated *in bello* proportionality. The military benefit from much of its bombing was small, but the damage to Iraqi civilians was immense. Thousands of them died during the war; many thousands more died after it from diseases caused by the lack of clean water. That was overkill, a degree of damage to non-combatants way out of proportion to its military rationale.

So the final verdict on the Gulf War is mixed. In its beginning, or by *ad bellum* criteria, it was morally just. It had a just cause, was necessary, and compared to its overall aims was proportionate. But in its conduct the Gulf War was unjust. The U.S. bombing of Iraq was excessive, violating either both the discrimination and proportionality rules or at least the second. This kind of mixed verdict wasn't much heard at the time. Supporters of the war tended to argue that it was just in all respects, opponents that it was thoroughly unjust. But often a mixed verdict is best, and it's a merit of just war theory to allow it. By including a number of conditions, the theory allows us to say that a given war satisfied some and violated others, and was therefore to be applauded in some respects and roundly condemned in others.

QUESTIONS FOR DISCUSSION

1. Was the U.S. bombing of Hiroshima and Nagasaki morally right or morally wrong? Was its moral status any different from that of a non-nuclear bombing killing exactly the same number of civilians?

2. Are there circumstances in which it could be right to bomb a nation's water purification and distribution systems? If so, what would those circumstances be?

3. Is it right that non-combatants have a special status in wartime, so they may not be directly targeted as military personnel can? What if the non-combatants voted for a government that began an unjust war and are cheering from the sidelines, while many of their nation's soldiers were conscripted into the military against their will?

Is the Death Penalty Cruel and Unusual?

*I*n October 1991, Joseph Kindler and Charles Ng were extradited to the United States to face, respectively, execution and a murder trial that may end in execution. Their lawyers had tried to block the extradition, arguing that exposing them to the death penalty would violate their guarantee under the Charter of Rights and Freedoms not to be subjected to "cruel and unusual treatment or punishment." In a narrow decision, the Supreme Court rejected this argument.

The ban on "cruel and unusual punishment" comes originally from the English Bill of Rights of 1689; it's also in the U.S. Constitution. There are two ways of arguing that it applies to capital punishment: that the death penalty is excessive or barbaric, and that it's not an effective means to the proper goal of punishment.

The simplest way of taking the first line is to say that capital punishment is excessive for any crime. Some opponents of the death penalty do say this, arguing that any deliberate killing is wrong.

But this principle implies, absurdly, that killing in self-defence is wrong. Imagine that attackers are coming at you with the clear intent to kill, and the only way you can save yourself is by killing them. If you kill them you do so deliberately, but isn't this your right?

Self-defence and punishment have similar functions. In the one case, you use force (a kind of coercion) to protect your rights. In the other, the state makes a threat (another kind of coercion) to protect your rights, saying that anyone who harms you will be harmed in turn. If coercion in general is allowed, making this threat is, and so is carrying it out.

A less sweeping argument is that capital punishment is excessive for some particular crime. And this argument is often persuasive. Maybe capital punishment would be an effective deterrent to shoplifting; if rigorously applied to shoplifters, it might eliminate the crime entirely. But it would surely be wrong — it would be cruel and unusual — to execute shoplifters: the penalty would be out of proportion to the crime. The U.S. Supreme Court has ruled that capital punishment for rape is unconstitutional on this ground. We should hope for similar reasoning from the Supreme Court of Canada.

But it's hard to apply this argument to capital punishment for murder. Here there's no disproportion between crime and punishment: a life is taken for a life. You do no more to criminals than they did to their victim.

The second argument is that capital punishment doesn't further the proper goal of punishment. If this goal is to prevent crimes, the argument says that capital punishment doesn't deter murder better than the alternative of life imprisonment.

Many studies have been done on the deterrent effect of capital punishment. Murder rates have been compared in American states with and without the death penalty, or in the same state before and after abolition. The studies are hard to interpret, but the judicious conclusion is that there's no evidence that capital punishment deters better than life imprisonment. There's no proof that it deters worse, but there's also no proof that it does a better job.

This is an excellent reason for legislators to vote against capital punishment. Considering the severity of capital punishment, we need positive grounds to endorse it. Lacking these grounds, Canadian MPs were right to reject it (again) in 1987.

But what's a good reason for legislators needn't be one for judges. It's not for judges to substitute their judgement for Parliament's on a matter of sociological fact, such as whether the death penalty deters. They can consider whether a law before them is rationally connected to its goal, but they should give legislators the benefit of the doubt.

Imagine that Parliament voted to reinstate capital punishment in 1987 and the Supreme Court was considering the constitutionality of this move. If the judges thought Parliament was mistaken about the deterrent effect of capital punishment, but reasonably so — the MPs were wrong on a subject where a reasonable person could be wrong — they would have to let the death penalty stand. Only if the error were one that no reasonable person could make would it be proper to correct it.

Capital punishment is wrong, but for a finely balanced reason: there's no positive evidence that it deters better than life imprisonment. And even this claim is contentious enough that reasonable people can dispute it.

Capital punishment should therefore be illegal in Canada, but not unconstitutional. We're right to have banned it, but it's not, in the constitutional sense, cruel and unusual.

QUESTIONS FOR DISCUSSION

1. If capital punishment doesn't deter murder better than life imprisonment, is it wrong to impose it?

2. If capital punishment did deter murder better than life imprisonment, would it be right to impose it?

3. How serious an argument against capital punishment is it that mistakes may be made and innocent people executed?

Part Ten

Virtues and Vices

Virtues are traits of character that make one act and feel properly; vices have the opposite effect. But it's not always clear what is a virtue or vice, and why. Is modesty a good trait or a bad one? What exactly is so nasty about envy? Can mere fantasies be morally bad? The essays in this part examine a number of issues about character, closing with a discussion of what it means to be, in the true sense, an intellectual.

Modesty Is a Mistake, but at Least Modest People Do Us a Favour

*O*ur moral thinking has its roots in the Jewish and Christian religions, but is trying to separate itself from them. This leads to some puzzling holdovers, such as the way we feel about modesty.

It's the Academy Awards, and the famous actor has just received the Oscar for best performance. But he doesn't give the standard acceptance speech (thanking the Academy, saying how surprised he is, listing several other people who really deserve the credit). Instead, he says: "My performance in this movie was damn good, clearly the best of the year. You couldn't have given the award to anyone else. I deserved it." How ungracious, we'd say, how un – Sally Fieldish, how arrogant. But what if everything the actor says is true?

Modesty makes sense given Christian beliefs, for then we all have lots to be modest about. If the doctrine of original sin is true, we're all essentially wicked. Even without this doctrine, on the scale that really counts our achievements are insignificant. Compared to the saints, to Jesus, to God, our virtues are as nothing.

But without religious beliefs there's no such scale, and some people really are good. To think, despite this, that they should be modest — should show and really have a humble opinion of themselves — is to demand that they be irrational. People are to believe dogmatically and against evidence that they're not good when they are. (Know thyself? No, be ignorant of thyself.)

Aristotle was a non-religious moralist, and he believed none of this. He thought a fully virtuous man (and for him it had to be a man) would be not modest, but proud. He would be good, know he was good, and demand to be treated as good. He'd be contemptuous of his inferiors and of little honours he thought unworthy of his dignity. Pride as Aristotle describes it strikes us today as offensive. But why? Should people be mistaken about their merits?

Modesty may be attractive partly because it counters a more common tendency people have — to overestimate themselves. In psychological experiments, subjects say the positive traits on a list are more true of them and their friends than the negative ones. They rate their own performances higher than neutral observers do, and say that while the areas they're good in are important, those they're bad in are not.

Over-rating ourselves in this way is psychologically beneficial. It protects our psyches when we perform badly and stimulates us to perform better. If we exaggerate our talents, we may work harder at developing them than if we weren't self-deceived. When our reach exceeds our grasp, we can end up grasping more.

But what's psychologically beneficial can also be ugly, and modesty can look good in comparison. In fact, some argue that modesty consists just in not overestimating oneself. Modest people don't have an irrationally low opinion of themselves; they just fail to have an irrationally high one.

If this were all that modesty involved, even Aristotle would applaud it. He wanted people to have accurate beliefs about themselves, and considered pride a vice in someone whose virtues didn't justify it.

But it's not clear that this is all we want in modesty. We think it seemly for even outstanding people to be publicly humble and downplay their merits. And since we don't like being lied to — we can't stand "false modesty" — this seems to require inaccurate self-assessments.

Perhaps we should think of modesty as a sacrifice. Modest people misunderstand themselves, and this makes their own lives worse. But it makes our lives easier. If successful people advertised their achievements, that would remind the rest of us of our failings. If they downplay the gap between us, we can more easily ignore it.

At the next Academy Awards there will be many humble acceptance speeches, and some, we can hope, will express real humility. We should accept this as a gift: people willfully misunderstanding their true nature to spare us the pain of really understanding ours.

QUESTIONS FOR DISCUSSION

1. Is it true that modesty as commonly understood involves having false beliefs about one's merits and achievements?

2. Do outstanding people owe anything to those who are less accomplished and would be pained by knowing how inferior they are?

3. Would a morally ideal person know in detail about his or her merits and virtues and take pleasure in them, or is it unseemly to be pleased by one's own good moral character?

Why Envy Is the Ugliest of the Seven Deadly Sins

*W*hen I was a teenager, I often didn't have a girlfriend. This bothered me, especially since so many of my friends did have girlfriends. The comparison rankled: me with no love life and everyone else in ecstasy.

I was envious, minding that I didn't have what other people had. And this strengthened my yearning to find a girlfriend: not only would this be good in itself (in your teens it seems supremely good), but it would stop me being the odd person out.

This wasn't a pretty motivation. It's not noble to want something more because someone else has it — or in extreme cases only because they have it. (Do you want a new car just because your neighbour bought one?) But sometimes my envy took an uglier form. Sometimes I'd realize that my romantic inferiority wasn't about to end in the best way, by my finding a girlfriend. So I'd secretly wish that it end in the second-best way, by other people's losing theirs. If I learned that someone's romance had broken up I'd feel sympathy, but I'd also get a nasty little pleasure knowing that now I wasn't alone. In a small part of me, I'd delight in misfortunes that brought others down to my level.

It's this second, spiteful side that makes envy such a nasty sin, perhaps the ugliest of the deadly seven.

The other sins are directed at something that in itself is good. Greed and selfishness aim at your happiness, which it's reasonable to pursue. Sloth goes for relaxation and gluttony for the pleasures of eating: each, again, something fine in moderation. The sin comes only in pursuing a good thing to excess.

But envy doesn't have a good object. It's purely negative, wishing misfortunes on others not for the sake of some benefit—you get nothing from it—but out of pure malice. This makes the existence of envy puzzling. If there's nothing in the emotion for you, why do you feel it?

Sometimes what looks like envy isn't. If you get 70 percent on a test at school, you don't yet know how well you did. If everyone else got 50, your performance was great; if they got 95, you did poorly. So, having got your test back, you may hope the class average is low rather than high. This isn't envy, just a natural expression of the desire to do well.

Some argue that all envy has this basis. You want to do well in life and to feel good about your achievements. But how worthy those achievements are depends on what others do. If you sometimes want them to do badly, it's because you want yourself to do well. Envy does have a good object that it wants to excess; it is like the other sins.

But this argument doesn't explain my envy of others' girlfriends. I didn't mind my loveless state because I thought it reflected badly on my skill or prowess; I didn't view dating as a contest. There were pleasures and experiences I wanted for their own sake; if I couldn't have them, I wanted others to go without too.

The argument also can't explain why, when I did have girlfriends, I wasn't jealous. Jealousy is like envy in caring about comparisons, but it starts from the superior position. Having what others don't have, it wants things to stay that way. It wants to be alone on top of the hill rather than have others stand beside it.

But when I had girlfriends I was generous and expansive: everyone should have delights like these! And I think this is a common pattern. Although we care a lot about comparisons when they make us look bad, we care less when they make us look good. Our tendency to envy isn't matched by a similar tendency to jealousy.

This is somewhat consoling: although spiteful in bad times, we're not so begrudging in good times. But it still leaves the ugly fact of envy.

When I look back on my teenage envy, it's with shame at its nastiness. If you feel envy, you have a good reason to envy the lucky (and finer) souls that are free of it. And when you've left it behind, you have no reason to be jealous.

QUESTIONS FOR DISCUSSION

1. Is envy a common emotion? If so, what makes it so common?

2. How does the essay distinguish between envy and jealousy? Is this a distinction worth making?

3. Are people who favour a more equal distribution of wealth and income motivated by
   envy—envy of those who have more than
   they do?

If You Want to Stop Procrastinating, Don't Put It Off until Tomorrow

*G*iven that we all procrastinate, why aren't we better at it? When we put off the work we really ought to be doing, why can't we at least do something enjoyable?

You're a university student with an essay due next week that you know you should start tonight. So when a friend calls with a really appealing idea — a night dancing at your favourite blues bar — you say you can't go, you've got too much work. But ...

It's after dinner and you're feeling a little tired, so you turn on the TV: you'll relax for fifteen minutes, then get to work. But YTV has a "Get Smart" rerun and, although the plot is lame, you watch to the end and somehow don't turn off on the half hour. Then there's "Cheers" and, well, you'll watch that until eight o'clock, when there'll still be lots of time for work.

At eight there's an NFL game, normally pretty boring, but you'll just see if this one team scores its touchdown. And so it goes until half past eleven, when you finally turn off the TV. You haven't done any work and you haven't really enjoyed anything you've watched. You've had far less fun, and accomplished no more, than if you'd gone out dancing.

This is what makes procrastination so damnable. Not only do we not do what's best, we often don't do what's second best. We waste our time doing something we'd never choose for its own sake.

Procrastination is a kind of weakness of will, of not doing what you know you ought. And it's hard to be weak-willed to your face, to admit openly that you're going to do something less good. That's what you would do if you went dancing: decide openly to put off your essay. But the TV is more devious. At no point in the evening do you decide to do no work. You're just watching for an extra fifteen minutes, and what's the serious harm in that?

It's this deviousness that makes procrastination so hard to shake. The how-to books are full of rational strategies: schedule your time, be disciplined, offer yourself rewards. But they're impotent against an enemy that works behind your back.

Sometimes you can beat procrastination by getting rid of what causes it, for example, a fear of failure. A project is important to your self-esteem and you're afraid of doing it badly. You put off starting because you don't want to face that failure or, more subtly, want to have an excuse when it happens. ("Of course I did badly; I started late.")

Here you can stop attaching so much importance to your work or lower unreasonably high standards. (If it isn't perfect it needn't be completely bad.) But not all cases are like this. There was no self-esteem involved when I put off staining my front steps for two months after they were built. And some projects really are important.

The way to beat a devious enemy is to be devious in return, to work behind its back as it works behind yours.

Picasso was such a productive artist because he went to his studio first thing every morning and started painting. Only after a long day's work was he free for drink, women, and philosophizing. The writers who are furthest from being "blocked" have a similar routine: three hours or 1500 words every morning, without fail. These writers don't offer themselves a reward every morning. ("Write now and you can play later.") They don't think at all. Whatever the day, regardless whether the work ahead of them is hard or easy, they just sit down and do it. They're on automatic pilot.

Routines beat procrastination because they don't let it get started: if you don't really make a choice you can't make a bad one. They make an end run around delay. But routines aren't created overnight. You have to develop them, and the question is when. ("In fifteen minutes.") As an extra incentive, you should remember: without routines you'll not only procrastinate but procrastinate badly. When you're not writing your essay or staining the steps you won't be out dancing, you'll be doing something as dull as watching reruns on TV.

QUESTIONS FOR DISCUSSION

1. Give some other examples of weakness of will — of not doing what you know is best. Can they be combatted in the same way as procrastination?

2. Is it depressing that sometimes we can only do what's best by not thinking about it? Would ideal agents not have to be so devious with themselves?

3. If TV networks and advertisers take advantage of our tendency to procrastination or weakness — if they structure their schedule so we'll find it harder to turn off — are they acting unethically?

Slim Pickings in a Society of Choosers

*O*rdering food in restaurants is a test (or at least a revelation) of character: it shows whether you're a picker, a chooser, or someone who can switch skilfully between the two.

We don't normally distinguish picking from choosing, but there's an important difference. You choose when you take one thing rather than another because you think there's a reason to do so. You pick when you do the same without thinking there's a reason.

Let's say you're shopping and buy chicken soup rather than tomato. If you do this because you think chicken soup is healthier, you're choosing — whether your reason's a good one or not. Of course, you can't buy just chicken soup; you have to buy a particular can. But there are many cans on the shelf, no one any better than the rest. When despite this, you take one, you pick.

Some philosophers think picking is impossible. This is the assumption behind the story of Buridan's ass, the donkey named after medieval philosopher Jean Buridan. Buridan's ass stands exactly midway between two indistinguishable piles of hay. Lacking a reason to go to one rather than the other, it starves to death. This might happen if the donkey had to choose, but why can't it pick and arbitrarily go left or right?

Mass production gives us many opportunities for picking and lots of evidence that we can do it. We don't stand frozen in supermarkets, forced to find a difference between one can of vegetable soup and its neighbour. Nor are we flummoxed by equally indistinguishable cassette tapes, TVs, or batteries.

Sometimes when we pick, we'd rather be choosing. For example, there's a story about a prisoner whose fate depends on selecting the door with a beautiful woman behind it rather than the one with a tiger. With no way to distinguish one door from the other, he can only pick, but he'd love to know enough to be choosing.

This is a general effect of knowledge: to turn picking situations into choosing ones. But you can go too far down this road—which brings us back to restaurants.

Faced with a menu, you don't want just to pick: there's useful information to apply. In Alberta, beef and pork are good bets, exotic seafood less so. Some wines go better with some dishes.

But many of us turn ordering into a test. We decide that there's a single best dish on the menu, or a single best series of dishes, and think it's up to our savoir-faire to discover it. This isn't sophisticated behaviour, it's neurotic. We're trying to choose past the point where there are grounds for doing so.

A perfectly rational person could switch deftly between choosing and picking. If there was an important decision and evidence relevant to it, they'd choose. If not, they'd pick. But few of us are like this. Edna Ullmann-Margalit and Sydney Morgenbesser, the philosophers who first wrote about picking and choosing, think that choosers and pickers are distinct personality types. Choosers like having reasons for what they do, and try to find them. They're refined and discriminating, but also pedantic and uptight. Pickers are nonchalant, carefree, uneducated, sloppy.

Children, surprisingly, are choosers. Given a plate of identical cookies, they'll pore over them seriously until a favoured Oreo is found, and woe betide a sibling who wants the same one.

In an age of mass production you'd expect us to go for picking, but we tend toward excessive choosiness. This is partly because of our desire for expertise, our desire to be better than our neighbours at distinguishing between wines, running shoes, and jazz records. But it also reflects the power of advertising.

The purpose of advertising is to replace picking with choosing. Untutored, we'd be able only to pick between brands or, at best, choose on the basis of price. Since companies don't like this, they highlight "special features" of their products to create preferences for them.

Sometimes this is useful: when products differ significantly and ads show us how they differ. But often we end up choosing when the sensible move would be to pick. There are taste differences between Coke and Pepsi, but they hardly justify the fanatical brand loyalty that is shown. One Pepsi ad showed a Greyhound driver deciding not to make his regular stop at a diner because the "Pepsi" before "Cola" on the neon sign had been turned off. Quite apart from its authoritarianism (don't the passengers get a vote?), the ad applauds behaviour that can only be described as neurotic.

Of two contrary vices, one can be more common and so more important to guard against. Since our temptation is excessive choosing, let's have a go at picking. Next time in a restaurant, let's relax, not bother, and say, "I'll have the duck, with some kind of red wine, and who cares about the vegetables?"

QUESTIONS FOR DISCUSSION

1. Would an ideal restaurant menu have a large number of items or only a few? Or would there be menus of different lengths for different customers?

2. Why do people care so much about being experts or connoisseurs about food, wine, music, and so on? Is the impulse a healthy one or not?

3. If advertisers take advantage of our desire to be choosers — if they create "brand loyalty" where brands are essentially the same, thereby causing us to waste money — are they acting unethically?

Is It Bad to Think Bad Thoughts?

*I*n 1976, Jimmy Carter told *Playboy* in an interview that he had committed "adultery in his heart" many times by looking on "a lot of women with lust." His confession drew titters from U.S. sophisticates, who thought this thinking was long behind them.

Mr. Carter had two ideas: that mere thoughts or imaginings can be morally wrong, and that they are wrong when they involve lust for someone other than your spouse.

The "mere" in "mere thoughts" is important. Often we find fantasies troubling because we think they express desires that can lead to action. This needn't be so, however: you can take pleasure in imagining something you'd never want in real life.

Lynne Segal, a British feminist, reports having sexual fantasies in which she is passive and humiliated, even though she doesn't want this from her real sex partners. It's hard to know how common this is, but it's possible. And Mr. Carter's first idea is that even when it happens —

when a fantasy won't become reality — the fantasy can be wrong.

This idea needs a little revision. To be wrong, an action must be voluntary, something you could prevent. Now, some fantasies are voluntary: you rent a video to stimulate them. But often both an imagined scene and your pleasure in it come unbidden into your mind. (This seems to happen to Mr. Carter and Ms. Segal.)

Although we can't say involuntary fantasies are wrong, we can say they are morally bad. They are morally regrettable even though, when they come, you aren't to blame. Behind this revised idea is a general principle: that it's bad to take pleasure in thoughts of whatever is wrong or bad. If something would be bad if it existed, enjoying it even in your mind shows an improper attitude.

Mr. Carter combines this principle with a traditional Christian sexual morality. He thinks adultery is bad and so condemns adulterous fantasy as bad. But the principle has wider application.

You may get a thrill imagining yourself torturing someone. Here you take pleasure in another person's pain and in your causing it. Since both of these are evil, your thoughts are evil. The principle can also be combined with non-traditional sexual moralities. Feminists do this in their distinction between erotica and pornography.

Feminists don't think all non-marital sex is wrong; if it involves mutual respect, it's fine. So they have no problems with fantasies of this kind of sex or with sexually explicit materials that stimulate them. In fact, a Calgary feminist puts on shows of her collection of erotica. What feminists object to is sex that is coercive or degrading. Films that present images of this type of sex and encourage pleasure in them are pornographic.

The issue here isn't censorship. You can think something is bad without thinking anyone has the

right to prevent it. Feminists who favour censorship (and not all do) use the different argument
that pornography, by affecting men's attitudes,
increases real violence against women. Even if we
don't buy this argument, we can find pornographic fantasies repellent.

To see this, imagine that pornography prevents
rape by siphoning off the energies that cause it.
Now there isn't a reason to censor pornography,
and there may be a reason to want it around. But
things are hardly ideal. Surely people are
depraved if they can only avoid real rape by
enjoying rape in their minds.

The pornography issue is said to make allies of
feminists and the fundamentalist right. This is
partly true and partly not. Feminists and the right
agree in disliking some sexual materials and perhaps wanting them banned. They disagree about
why the materials are bad: the right because they
are sexually explicit, feminists because they
endorse degradation. But at the deepest level,
they share Mr. Carter's first idea: that it's bad to
take pleasure in whatever is bad.

Does this idea seem unfamiliar? If so, it's partly
because we're bad at abstraction, at seeing how
two opposed positions can share an underlying
principle. It's also because we throw out babies
with the bathwater.

The idea of "sins of the heart" has long been
associated with traditional sexual morality.
(Feminism is still a minority position.) Many
people who have abandoned this morality think
they should also give up the idea that thoughts
can be morally evaluated.

This is a mistake. We can change our view of
what's bad but still think fantasizing about what's
bad is bad. If we do, we'll have lots to ponder in a
culture whose entertainment industries repeatedly
encourage fantasies of beating up, killing, or
humiliating other people.

QUESTIONS FOR DISCUSSION

1. If it is bad to take pleasure in imagining things that are bad, is it also bad to take pleasure in really existing bad things, such as really existing pain? Is it worse?

2. Is there an important distinction between pornography and erotica? If so, does the distinction turn on the typical states of mind of those who enjoy the two?

3. If you are happy when the villain gets killed at the end of a Hollywood movie, are you having a morally bad fantasy?

Hypocrisy: Not All It's Cracked Down to Be

I don't want to defend famous hypocrites like TV evangelist Jimmy Swaggart and former Israeli Prime Minister Yitzhak Shamir. But hypocrisy gets a worse press than it deserves. Its common forms aren't that terrible, and it's never that morally important.

Hypocrites don't walk their talk: they profess one thing and do another. There's a conflict between the moral principles they say they believe in and those they actually follow. In the standard picture, hypocrites know about this conflict and plan it. They don't believe the fine words they spout, but use them, cynically, to manipulate other people.

The famous literary hypocrites fit this picture. Dickens's Uriah Heep keeps saying what a "very 'umble servant" he is while plotting to steal his boss's money. Tartuffe in Moliere's play uses a pose of piety to seduce religious women.

This deliberate hypocrisy is indeed repellent. It's bad enough that hypocrites do something wrong, such as stealing. On top of that, they lie about their moral beliefs and use the lie to trick other people. But I doubt if many of us could manage all this: it takes too much self-control. And what we more commonly do is less purely awful.

In a common form of hypocrisy, you believe the moral principles you state and wish you could live up to them. But you can't — you're weak-willed. You do, against your will, what you know and say is wrong.

Mr. Swaggart may be like this: he may sincerely think it's wrong to spend time with prostitutes but be unable to stop. And can't we all sympathize with weakness?

Mr. Swaggart isn't blameless. He may not lie about his moral beliefs, but he isn't completely open about himself. His public statements encourage the belief that he's sexually pure, and he doesn't give the extra information that would show us otherwise. This may be partly due to self-deception. He may believe that his weakness is temporary and will soon be overcome. Once it's gone, who will need to know about it?

Sometimes self-deception plays a larger role. In another kind of hypocrisy, you don't even notice the conflict between your principles and your actions. You persuade yourself, despite the evidence, that you're living the ideals you preach. Mr. Shamir may be like this. How else could he condemn others simply as "terrorists" when he himself practised terrorism in the 1940s?

Self-deceiving hypocrisy may seem less deserving of sympathy than the weak-willed kind — there's no inner struggle. But that's because the inner enemy is stronger. Your desires have overcome not only your will but also your intellect.

Besides often being understandable, hypocrisy isn't morally important. For consider another literary hypocrite, Huckleberry Finn. Huck Finn thinks runaway slaves should be caught and turned in — they're their masters' property. But despite prodding from his "conscience," he helps his slave friend Jim escape to freedom. Here there's no temptation to say the conflict between Huck's principles and actions is wrong. Since he's learned the principles from an unjust society, violating them is all to the good.

In Huck's case, what matters is what he does, not what he says. And that's true generally: deeds count, not words or their relationship to deeds.

Caring too much about hypocrisy reveals a lack of confidence about moral judgements. You can't argue convincingly that someone's done wrong, or expect others to buy your argument, so you retreat to a charge of hypocrisy: "They're not doing what they themselves say they should."

Our public debates often turn on charges of hypocrisy. We like jumping on budget-cutting politicians who raise their salaries, Marxists who live in big houses, or environmentalists whose cars leak oil. But maybe these people are just weak-willed or self-deceived or not doing everything Hercules would to advance an ideal.

There's another option: someone isn't living by a principle they espouse because they realize deep down, that it's flawed. But then pointing out the hypocrisy should be just the start of an argument showing *why* the principle is flawed.

Too often we use the word "hypocrite!" not just to start but to end a moral argument. That means we're not really addressing issues of right and wrong. It means, in fact, that we're only pretending to address these issues — in a way, another kind of hypocrisy.

QUESTIONS FOR DISCUSSION

1. Why is hypocrisy thought to be such an ugly or awful vice?

2. If people violate their professed ethical principles because of weakness of will or self-deception, should we sympathize with them or condemn them?

3. How much should we care if budget-cutting politicians raise their own salaries or environmentalists' cars leak oil?

Competitiveness:
Should We Play for Love or Play to Win?

*Y*ou probably don't consider Don Cherry a thinker, but he has a subtle philosophy of hockey. He thinks you play best when you try as hard as possible to win: skating, shooting, checking, grinding, giving all you've got for victory.

This isn't the crude view stated by former Green Bay Packers coach Vince Lombardi: "Winning isn't everything; it's the only thing." Mr. Cherry realizes that what matters is how you play the game. But he equates playing well with *trying* to win — even bending the rules to beat your opponent.

Like all philosophers' views, Mr. Cherry's is controversial. If he applauds competition, an opposed view decries it. This view has been applied to hockey by Ontario philosopher John McMurtry. Against the model of competitive hockey, Professor McMurtry holds up an ideal of "free hockey," based on shinny or pick-up hockey, the game played on ponds and outdoor rinks across Canada. In shinny, the players are whoever shows up, and teams are chosen arbitrarily. No one cares about winning; no one even keeps score. People play just for the love of the game. It's shinny, Professor McMurtry says, that's hockey at its best, not Mr. Cherry's competitive game.

Latent here is a larger issue. In our culture we compete for many things: grades, jobs, lovers, prestige. Is this competitiveness a good thing? To settle the issue as Canadians, we should first get it right about hockey.

Professor McMurtry has many objections to organized hockey. The game has an authoritarian structure, with coaches giving orders and players obeying; participants wear armour from head to toe; teams are separated from each other, cheering only their own members' good play and not their opponents'; there are cheating and violence — spearing, slashing, fighting. He's less forthcoming, though, about the sins of shinny.

Consider padding. It not only allows body-checking but also protects you against the puck. Because of this, shinny without pads needs a rule against raising the puck. But this means goals can only be scored from within 1m of the net, which eliminates two-thirds of the dimension of offence.

Also missing is the whole dimension of defence. Defensive play, for example, back-checking, is the ugly duckling of hockey, hard to love for itself. Since it's vital to winning, though, teams who want to win practise it. But you don't find it in shinny. This further impoverishes the offence in shinny. The offensive skill you need in a game depends on the defensive tenacity you face. Stickhandling around a player who can't body-check you is relatively easy, beating one who's playing the man is an achievement.

In fact, shinny lacks the very qualities Professor McMurtry values: co-operation and equality.

Shinny is a hot dog's game, featuring one-on-one rushes and selfishness. Without the defensive play born of trying to win, there's no need for teamwork. Add back-checking, and players have to pass the puck.

Shinny is also anti-egalitarian. If you're not naturally talented—you're not a great skater—you can't make big rushes and you have little role in shinny. But in organized hockey you can compensate with brains. Anticipate the play, get to the right spot, and if your teammates want to win, they'll feed you the puck.

This doesn't mean there's nothing wrong with competitive hockey, especially as played in the NHL. (Mr. Cherry's videos of hockey fights are disgusting.) You can't love the institutionalized hatred, the desire to see an opponent lose and make him feel it. But sometimes you can't get good things without bad things.

It would be nice if we could always do the best thing from the best motive, playing the most skilful hockey without wanting anyone to lose. But we aren't like that. Often we need extra motives for excellence, and what comes with these motives isn't always attractive.

There's a conflict, for us, between two ideals: of the amateur and the professional. The amateur plays only for love of the game and therefore doesn't play very well. Professionals care about winning and therefore play better, but their competitiveness gives them an uglier character.

The conflict may sometimes be avoidable. After her silver medal skate at the Calgary Olympics, Elizabeth Manley said she had to learn not to think of winning but to do her routine just for its own sake. If she's right, in skating the best performance does require the best motive.

But sports like hockey are different. There, excellence requires viewing your play partly or mainly as a means to a goal that does down other people. Are the benefits of this worth the costs? Is the improved performance worth the deformation of character? Let's put it this way. If Canada played only shinny, it would never have produced a battler like Dave Semenko, and that might be a good thing. But then it would never have produced Wayne Gretzky, either.

QUESTIONS FOR DISCUSSION

1. Is there something admirable in itself about trying to win — about giving all you've got for victory in a sport?

2. Phil Esposito said the 1972 Canada – Russia hockey series was the only time in his life he would have killed to win a hockey game. Should this make Canadians who remember the series look back on it more fondly or with horror?

3. Outside sports — in school, business life, and personal relationships — do the benefits of competitiveness outweigh its costs, or is it on balance undesirable?

Why Intellectuals Care about the Flintstones

*I*n an SCTV sketch called "Philosophy Today," a group of academics sit around a TV studio waiting for their discussion show to begin. As the cameras roll, the moderator announces the topic for the day: "Were 'The Flintstones' a rip-off of 'The Honeymooners?'" A heated discussion ensues.

The sketch is hilarious, but also deeply insightful. A real intellectual would want to know, would be excited to learn, that "The Flintstones" *were* a rip-off of "The Honeymooners."

What is an intellectual? Some people think intellectuals are distinguished by their interest in certain highbrow subjects. Intellectuals like poetry, painting, and architecture. They talk about international and national (though never local) politics. They think no dinner party complete without some discussion of opera, and get annoyed when you interrupt to ask whether they don't think Fred Flintstone was modelled on Ralph Cramden and Barney on Ed Norton.

These aren't intellectuals, just highbrows. Real intellectuals differ, not in the subjects they follow, but in the approach they take to any subject. They want to know or understand everything. They care about poetry and architecture, but they also look at the ordinary world around them.

Understanding means knowing generalizations, and real intellectuals look for generalizations on all subjects. They try to spot trends in advertising and popular television. They wonder whether any unifying characteristics distinguish U.S. sports from those popular in other countries. They debate the hypothesis that as you mount through the social classes, the writing on "legible clothing" (clothing with words on it) gets progressively smaller and eventually disappears.

Intellectuals want to unify information. They know the greatest scientific advances occur when what appeared to be distinct phenomena are seen to follow from the same laws, as when Newton gave the same explanation of the motions of heavenly bodies and objects on Earth. Something similar happens when you see the parallels between Wilma's relationship to Fred and Alice's to Ralph: smarter than, exasperated by, but always lovey-dovey and forgiving at the end of the show.

Intellectuals follow popular culture, but in its social context. They find it curious that in the 1950s, when TV was a luxury of the well-to-do, many popular programs featured working-class characters, whereas in the 1960s, when TV ownership became universal, the subjects were almost exclusively middle class.

This is reflected in "The Flintstones" and "The Honeymooners." Like Ralph and Ed, Fred and Barney are working men, with ordinary jobs and interests. But where Ralph and Ed live in apartments, Fred and Barney, in a concession to the 1960s, have detached houses in the suburbs.

Even when they discuss the same subjects, highbrows and real intellectuals do so differently. Highbrows think discussing, say, politics intellectually means making lots of references to various Great Dead Political Thinkers. They are demons of quotesmanship. In their writing, "Spinoza said" follows "de Tocqueville remarked" follows "Burke pointed out."

Real intellectuals don't do this. They've read the great philosophers, but they don't need to advertise this fact. And they don't like to bludgeon people with famous names. They know that what made the great thinkers great was not their snappy remarks, but their extended arguments, and that what you need to persuade someone honestly is also an argument — perhaps extended, perhaps complex, but in straightforward language and without needless references.

Once again, it is content versus style. Highbrows think being intellectual means knowing certain facts. For real intellectuals it means thinking logically, precisely, and with an eye to important generalizations.

A persistent hawker of highbrowism is Woody Allen. In his movies, a woman is often transformed into an intellectual by a man — in *Annie Hall* by Mr. Allen himself, in *Hannah and Her Sisters* by that awful sculptor. In each case the process is the same: the man recommends some books, the woman reads them and, presto, she's a thinker. At the end she gives full credit for her transformation to her (now ex-) lover.

There's no hint in these movies that reading big books isn't enough. Mr. Allen doesn't consider that you have to challenge the arguments you read, and that if you do, the credit for what you learn goes to you, not to whoever compiled your booklist.

Highbrows want big reforms in education. They want students to stop listening to rock'n'roll and read a series of set Great Books, works approached with reverence as stores of useful quotations and eternal truths. Real intellectuals also want students to read great books, but in the way their authors wanted: as presenting arguments that need to be probed as carefully for weaknesses as for insights, not accepted on faith.

Highbrowism is dangerous, because it erects unnecessary barriers. It discourages would-be intellectuals from addressing ordinary people and creates resentment of the intellectuals' airs. Highbrows want nothing to do with Fred Flintstone and Ralph Cramden, and Fred and Ralph would want nothing to do with them. But real intellectuals care about life in Bedrock and at the bus company, as about anything they can appreciatively understand.

QUESTIONS FOR DISCUSSION

1. Is all knowledge equally worth having and of equal intellectual value, for example, lists of Stanley Cup winners versus fundamental laws of the universe?

2. How much have you done to prove or support an opinion when you've quoted a famous writer who believed it?

3. At your next dinner party, will you discuss opera?

READER REPLY CARD

We are interested in your reaction to *Principles: Short Essays on Ethics*, Second Edition, by Thomas Hurka. You can help us to improve this book in future editions by completing this questionnaire.

1. What was your reason for using this book?
   - ❏ university course
   - ❏ college course
   - ❏ continuing education course
   - ❏ professional development
   - ❏ personal interest
   - ❏ other

2. If you are a student, please identify your school and the course in which you used this book.

3. Which chapters or parts of this book did you use? Which did you omit?

4. What did you like best about this book? What did you like least?

5. Please identify any topics you think should be added to future editions.

6. Please add any comments or suggestions.

7. May we contact you for further information?
   Name: _____
   Address: _____
   _____
   Phone: _____
   E-mail: _____

(fold here and tape shut)

0116870399-M8Z4X6-BR01

Larry Gillevet
Director of Product Development
HARCOURT BRACE & COMPANY, CANADA
55 HORNER AVENUE
TORONTO, ONTARIO
M8Z 9Z9